HOWARD HANSON
IN THEORY AND PRACTICE

Recent Titles in
Contributions to the Study of Music and Dance

HOWARD HANSON
IN THEORY AND PRACTICE

Allen Cohen

Contributions to the Study of Music and Dance, Number 66

Westport, Connecticut
London

Library of Congress Cataloging-in-Publication Data

Cohen, Allen (Allen Laurence)
    Howard Hanson in theory and practice / Allen L. Cohen
      p.   cm. — (Contributions to the study of music and dance, ISSN 0193–9041 ; no. 66)
    Includes bibliographical references (p.) and index.
    ISBN 0–313–32135–3 (alk. paper)
    1. Hanson, Howard, 1896– —Contributions in music theory. 2. Hanson, Howard,
1896– —Criticism and interpretation. 3. Hanson, Howard, 1896– Harmonic materials of
modern music. I. Title. II. Series.
  ML410.H1825C64 2004
   780′.92—dc22   2003057979

British Library Cataloguing in Publication Data is available.

Library of Congress Catalog Card Number: 2003057979
ISBN: 0–313–32135–3
ISSN: 0193–9041

First published in 2004

Praeger Publishers, 88 Post Road West, Westport, CT 06881
An imprint of Greenwood Publishing Group, Inc.
www.praeger.com

Printed in the United States of America

Contents

Acknowledgments

Many people have helped me in the writing of this book. I thank
Joseph N. Straus for his generous help in critiquing the manuscript,
and for guiding and encouraging my explorations into some of the
darker corners of musical set theory. I am also grateful to John M.
Graziano for his patience and guidance, and to Philip Lambert for
valuable suggestions, during earlier stages of the writing. In addition, Steven L. Rosenhaus and Beverly Chaney helped me to make
improvements in the manuscript; John Cinco did beautiful scans of
several pages; and John Beck, who oversaw book production, was of
immense assistance.

I am grateful to many members of the Eastman School of Music
community, past and present, for conversations and information—
especially Ruth T. Watanabe, Robert Morris, Vincent Lenti, John
Beck, Robert Gauldin, William Francis McBeth, and David Russell Williams. I also thank Mary Lynn Carroll for her gracious
help in clearing up some mysteries about the life and work of Robert
V. Sutton.

I owe a special debt of gratitude to two people. Marilyn Plain,
currently catalog librarian with the Rochester (New York) Public
Library, who catalogued the Howard Hanson manuscripts held by
the Sibley Music Library of the Eastman School of Music at the
University of Rochester, graciously made available to me all the
necessary research materials, and shared her knowledge of the
genesis and development of the works discussed. David Peter
Coppen, Special Collections Librarian at the Sibley Music Library,

was in all ways the most well-informed, assiduous and generous librarian for whom any researcher could ask. He went far beyond the call of duty in helping me to locate and examine relevant materials of all kinds.

While a Selected Bibliography appears at the back of the book, I wish in particular to acknowledge my debts to David Russell Williams's *Conversations with Howard Hanson*, which first gave me the idea for this book and provided many insights into Hanson's thoughts about theory and composition, and to James E. Perone's *Howard Hanson: A Bio-Bibliography*, an indispensable resource. Also helpful were two doctoral dissertations, Robert C. Monroe's "Howard Hanson: American Music Educator" and Andrea Sherlock Kalyn's "Constructing a Nation's Music: Howard Hanson's American Composers' Concerts and Festivals of American Music, 1925–71." To every extent possible, I have independently verified the accuracy of my sources. While I hope to have corrected some errors in each of the above, I have undoubtedly perpetuated some others— and perhaps added a few of my own—for which I take full responsibility, and solicit corrections from readers.

Finally I thank my parents, Harold and Diana Cohen, and my wife, Beverly Chaney, for their support and love during the long gestation of this book.

Chapter 1

Introduction

A composer who makes an original contribution to music theory provides an unusual opportunity to observe both the analytical and creative aspects of a single mind, and the various ways in which they interact. While most musicians would probably think of such names as Jean-Philippe Rameau, Arnold Schoenberg, Paul Hindemith, Milton Babbitt, and George Perle in this context, another member of this small company is Howard Hanson (1896–1981), an American whom few, even among musicians, know as a theorist.

In his lifetime, Hanson was among the most prominent of American musicians as educator, conductor, and composer. He helped to raise the Eastman School of Music to national renown as its director for forty years, and as a teacher of two generations of American composers. He was a highly-regarded conductor and champion of American music, whose recordings continue to be reissued more than twenty years after his death. One of the few American composers to have an opera commissioned and premiered by the Metropolitan Opera Company (*Merry Mount*, 1934), he won the Pulitzer Prize for music in 1944, and was awarded an abundance of commissions, prizes, and honors. His reputation, however, like those of many twentieth-century composers whose music remained tonally-oriented and Romantic in spirit, went into eclipse for several decades after World War II, an eclipse from which it has only recently begun to emerge. Even now he is surprisingly unknown and undiscussed for a twentieth-century American musician with a long list of prizes and achievements.

Among those achievements was the development of the first complete system of classification of every possible collection of pitches in the chromatic scale, which was presented in a book entitled *Harmonic Materials of Modern Music: Resources of the Tempered Scale*, hereinafter referred to as *Harmonic Materials*.[1] In this book Hanson also showed ways of deriving larger collections from smaller ones (and vice versa), and demonstrated significant relationships among such collections. Hanson's theoretical system anticipated, in many significant ways, the standard formulations of musical set theory as presented in the works of Allen Forte and other writers during the 1960s and afterward.

In a series of interviews conducted by a former composition student in 1978, Hanson said that he had worked on his system for many years before *Harmonic Materials* was published, and that all of his later pieces were influenced by this system.[2] One of my primary goals in this book is to test that assertion—to examine the connections, the mutual or reciprocal relations, between Hanson's theory and his compositional practice. The theory is expounded in *Harmonic Materials* and related writings. The practice is exemplified, first by two pieces that Hanson wrote in order to demonstrate aspects of his theory, and second by a number of more typical works written before and after the period (approximately 1935 to 1950) during which he formulated the theory. A combination of approaches, both analytical and musicological, will be used in the course of the book, in order to illuminate the relationship between Hanson's theory and his composition: evaluation of the theory and its presentation in *Harmonic Materials*; analysis of scores by Hanson, to verify the influence of the theory; and examination of Hanson's sketches and other writings, to supplement the study of his scores and to shed light on both the development of the theory and his method(s) of composition.[3]

Although a comparison of Hanson's theory and practice is my main intent, this book has several additional aims. One is to summarize Hanson's theory concisely in a new and accessible book. This is particularly desirable since *Harmonic Materials* is difficult to find or obtain, and since relatively few people, even among theorists, have been able (or willing) to take the time necessary to read it. Another goal is to present the first scholarly study of any of Hanson's music to appear in book form. In addition, by indicating the extent of Hanson's achievements in theory—achievements for which he has received little acknowledgment—I hope to redress the balance to some extent.[4]

To help clarify the context and background of the theory in Hanson's life and works—and because this multifaceted musician had a powerful impact on many aspects of American music in the twentieth century as composer, conductor, teacher, administrator, and advocate—I have endeavored to present an account of his life and career that corrects many of the factual errors that have crept into published accounts, and to provide the most complete biography of Hanson yet to see print. This biographical overview appears in Chapter 2. In Chapter 3, I summarize the theory as presented in *Harmonic Materials*. (The question has been raised whether the material presented in *Harmonic Materials* should be called a "system" and not a "theory."[5] In discussions of that material in this book, I will use the terms "system" and "theory" interchangeably: first for convenience, as most theorists usually do, and second because, no matter what else one may say about it, *Harmonic Materials* is a work that at least deals with music theory.)

Hanson made three main claims for his theory. The first was that it provided a system of classification for every possible collection of pitch classes in the chromatic scale. The second was that it was an effective technique for the analysis of any music written using the chromatic scale. The third claim was that it could serve as a melodic and harmonic resource for composers.

In Chapter 4, I describe the theory's development and publication in the context of a brief chronology of the attempts to develop a comprehensive theory of tonal relations. I follow this with an evaluation of Hanson's claim as to the comprehensiveness and utility of the system, considering the strengths and weaknesses of the theory and its presentation, particularly in comparison to musical set theory. In Chapter 5, I evaluate Hanson's claim that his theory offers an effective tool for musical analysis.

In Chapter 6, in consideration of his further claim that the theory offers to composers new harmonic and melodic resources, and ways of deriving further resources from any given material, I analyze two pieces by Hanson that were explicitly written, at least in part, to demonstrate aspects of his theory. These pieces are: *For the First Time* (1963), a suite for orchestra (or piano) in twelve movements, each of which uses a different pitch-class set (or "sonority," in Hanson's terminology) with five or more elements as its compositional basis; and *Young Person's Guide to the Six-Tone Scale* (1971–72), a suite for piano and wind ensemble in thirty-five short movements, each of which uses a different six-element pitch-class set (or, in Hanson's terminology, "hexad" or "six-tone scale"). I also examine sketches for the two works and other written or recorded comments of Hanson's, to illuminate his method of composition for these pieces, and to see whether this method can have any relevance to the composition of pieces without such "didactic" intent.[6]

Following this line of thought further, in Chapter 7 I examine a number of major works written by Hanson after he had formulated his theory, to see the nature and degree of the influence, if any, that his theory had on their composition. For further light on this question, I make use of sketches for these and other works, as well as relevant remarks Hanson made in interviews and other writings outside of *Harmonic Materials*.

Finally, in Chapter 8, I attempt to answer the broader question of the degree of influence exerted by Hanson's theory upon his later compositional style. Then, by examining portions of several early Hanson works, I suggest an answer to the converse but perhaps equally interesting question: the degree of influence, if any, exerted by his earlier compositional style upon the origin and development of his theory.

Howard Hanson created a substantial number of works embodying craftsmanship, power, and beauty of a high order. His best music has spoken to, and touched the hearts of, more people than that of any but a handful of other American composers. As this book will show, in his own idiosyncratic way he also developed a comprehensive theoretical system that revealed an impressive amount of information about tonal relations, and revealed much of it before anyone else. For all of these reasons, an understanding of the relationship between his theory and his practice is worth pursuing.

Chapter 2

The Background: Hanson's Life and Career

CHILDHOOD AND EARLY CAREER

Howard Harold Hanson was born in Wahoo, a small town in eastern Nebraska about thirty miles north of the capital city of Lincoln, on October 28, 1896. Wahoo, the county seat of Saunders County, had at that time a population of less than two thousand, which has doubled in the last century. It was and still is a farm town, which was settled mostly by Czech Catholic and Swedish Lutheran immigrants. Surrounded by broad fields, it is dominated by a single large grain silo, and by a large billboard on a prominent corner of Highway 77 that celebrates the little town as the "City of Opportunity" and commemorates the "five famous men" who were born there: movie mogul Darryl F. Zanuck, baseball Hall of Fame member Sam Crawford, Nobel Prize-winning geneticist George W. Beadle, artist C. W. Anderson—and Howard Hanson, "Music Composer." Today Hanson's childhood home, a white two-story house at the corner of 12th and Linden Streets, is listed in the National Register of Historic Places, and is open to the public as part of the Saunders County Museum, restored to look much as it did when Hanson grew up there.

Hanson was an only child—an older brother had died before he was born—and he remained close to his parents, Hans and Hilma, for their entire lives. They had both been born in Sweden, and as a child Howard spoke Swedish as well as English. Like many other Scandinavian immigrants in the area, both parents were Luthans, active in their local church, and as a boy Hanson considered a career in the Lutheran ministry. (When he married later in life, he converted to his wife's Presbyterianism.) Although he never pursued the church as a career, religion remained important to him—in later life he would occasionally act as a substitute preacher at his church—and religious ideals and images are prominent in his writings and speeches, as well as in his compositions. He often spoke and wrote about music in almost mystical terms, as not only an aesthetic but a spiritual force, calling it "the language of the human spirit" and "a divinely great art . . . which is a part of infinity itself," and he referred to musicians as "evangelists of the art."[7] His father, who had no musical training, owned and ran a hardware store; his mother, a housewife, had studied voice and piano, and went on to study counterpoint after he was born. When her only son showed musical aptitude at an early age, she encouraged him and began to teach him piano, studies which continued at Luther College, a two-year Lutheran institution in Wahoo.[8] He began to compose and to study the cello, performing as a cellist in a high school string quartet and a college orchestra; he put himself through college by playing cello and piano, and then by conducting, on the "Chautauqua circuit" during his summer vacations and on one winter tour. Before he left he was assisting the manager in running the Chautauqua organization, and he later claimed that during these summers he had become friendly with William Jennings Bryan, who helped to improve his writing skills.

He was precocious and, as he later put it, "very ambitious." He was the valedictorian of his high school class—although, he would characteristically hasten to add, there were only thirteen students in the class. Even before he finished high school, he had already graduated from Luther College. He attended the School of Music of the University of Nebraska at Lincoln for the year 1912–13, then went to New York, where he stayed with his mother's brother, a successful actor, who became fond of him and later left him considerable bequests of money and real estate. Here he studied for another year at the Institute of Musical Art, which was incorporated into the Juilliard School a few years later. His studies at the Institute included counterpoint with the eminent pedagogue Percy Goetschius, and piano with James Friskin. As he would later recall with amusement, he was a promising enough pianist that Frank Damrosch, director of the Institute, once asked him why he was wasting his time with "futile efforts in composition" when he had the potential to become a great concert pianist. (In later years he made occasional appearances as a piano soloist in his own works.) During this time he completed what may have been his first orchestral piece, a two-movement suite entitled *Night and Dawn*, which he conducted in Wahoo in the summer of 1914.

With the aid of a teaching fellowship and tuition remission, Hanson then went on to Northwestern University, where he studied with Peter Christian Lutkin and Arne Oldberg. He later recalled that at Northwestern he had experimented with microtonal music by tuning two old pianos a quarter-tone apart and writing a piece for them. He also wrote a senior thesis entitled "Upon Temperament and Scale-Construction."[9] He soon lost interest in microtonal experimentation, however. As he put it late in life, in a comment that perhaps reflects the significance of his theoretical work in his composition, "the ordinary chromatic scale still offers such huge opportunities . . . that I would be perfectly willing to spend a couple more lifetimes working in the chromatic scale and not feel that I was being hemmed in."[10] He received a Bachelor of Music degree from Northwestern in 1916, when he was nineteen years old. (Although later he was often called "Dr. Hanson," the three dozen doctoral degrees he received were all honorary.)

He advanced as a teacher even more rapidly than he had as a student. His first position was head of the theory department in the Conservatory of Music and Art at the College of the Pacific in San Jose, California (which later became the University of the Pacific). He was appointed dean of the Conservatory three years later, at the age of twenty-two. From the beginning, Hanson displayed a prodigious energy and industry that he maintained for the rest of his career. In May 1921 he initiated a Festival of American Music at the College of the Pacific, a successful series of four concerts of new works, including an orchestral program with the Los Angeles Philharmonic in which Hanson conducted his *Symphonic Rhapsody*, Opus 14. (This Festival is not to be confused with the similar Festival of American Music that Hanson instituted in Rochester, New York, ten years later.) During this time he also had the opportunity to conduct the San Francisco Symphony in his *Symphonic Legend*, op. 8. Through these and other activities he made contacts with many musicians on the West Coast, and also began to supplement his income by ghost-writing and arranging popular tunes for a New York songwriter for $50 each, a clandestine activity which continued for several years.[11]

Like other young American men of the time, he seems to have enjoyed speculating about new scientific discoveries and tinkering with inventions in his backyard. In addition to his teaching and composition, Hanson produced several other creations during this time that show an early and lifelong interest in the systematic treatment of theoretical issues, and in the use of scientific methods in conjunction with music. He invented a machine to analyze the formant or overtone distribution of singing voices, which he hoped would help singing teachers to diagnose vocal problems, and shortly afterward he developed an apparatus to show overtones optically.[12] He also published an article in *Musical America* in which he criticized the current state of music theory for being "empirical" but not "scientific," and for failing to distinguish between rules based on tradition and true laws of acoustics. Near the end of the article he asserted, "The theorist should not be in the rearguard of the musical army as a mere recorder of musical progress. He should be a pioneer. . . . It is his duty to investigate carefully nature's laws and point out where man may tread in full accord with the principles of nature."[13] Soon afterward, he developed a series of tests that he claimed could measure the various aspects of a student's musical talent, based on the ideas of Carl Seashore, and later he conducted experiments on the emotional associations evoked in test subjects by harmonies of various types.[14] Throughout his career he continued to have a strong interest in both the acoustics and the psychology of music; years later he would insist that the Eastman School add courses in acoustics to its curriculum. After his time at the College of the Pacific, he does not seem to have pursued his inventing career quite as intently, apparently because he was too busy rather than because he had lost interest. Even in 1938, in the midst of his tenure as head of the Eastman School of Music, he helped to develop a device called a "recordograph" that permitted the recording of high fidelity performances from a number of venues at the Eastman School onto $33^1/_3$ rpm acetate discs.[15]

In 1921, when Hanson had served as dean at the College of the Pacific for two years, he applied for the first Prix de Rome in composition from the American Academy in Rome. (The prize had been offered in the previous year but had not been awarded.) He won the prize, and received with it a fellowship to the American Academy. With Leo Sowerby, who had been given a fellowship but not the prize, and Randall Thompson, who won the prize a year later, Hanson was given the chance to create, study, and travel for three years, free from financial pressures. There was no course of study; the fellows' time was to be spent composing and travelling through Europe, and Hanson took full advantage of the opportunity. He travelled to his parents' home town in Sweden as well as to England, Scotland, Germany, Switzerland, Austria, Italy, and France, where he visited Nadia Boulanger's studio and met Aaron Copland. The young Midwesterner also took advantage of opportunities to meet and hobnob with Italian aristocrats as well as wealthy young ladies and famous musicians visiting from America. While at the Academy,

Hanson performed at the piano and conducted the Augusteo Orchestra in concerts of his works and those of the other Academy fellows.

Although he had no formal course of study in Rome, he did ask for and receive advice from Ottorino Respighi, in the period after Respighi had written his most famous works, *Fontane di Roma* and *Pini di Roma*. Respighi also allowed Hanson to attend rehearsals and performances of his orchestral concerts. Hanson later felt that Respighi's influence on him had been primarily in terms of instrumentation and orchestral textures; in addition to Respighi's teacher Rimsky-Korsakov, he identified Holst and Wagner as compositional influences at this time. During this period he also studied Gregorian chant, the medieval modes, and the vocal works of Palestrina with great interest. He later considered Palestrina to be the "biggest single influence" on his composition, and credited his study of Palestrina's works, in editions using the original clefs, as having been the foundation of his legendary prowess at sight-reading.[16] During this time the English conductor Albert Coates, another acquaintance from Rome, introduced Hanson to a number of English composers. Hanson was particularly impressed with the support given by British musical organizations to new British music.[17]

While at the American Academy, Hanson also met Walter Damrosch, who had been on the jury for the Prix de Rome, and was conductor of the New York Symphony Society (one of the two orchestras that merged several years later to become the present-day New York Philharmonic). Damrosch looked at the score for Hanson's most recent work, a tone poem for orchestra and chorus entitled *North and West*, Opus 22, and promised Hanson to conduct its premiere in New York City with the New York Symphony in February 1924. (Shortly before the premiere Damrosch gave Hanson the chance to conduct the New York performance himself.) In Rome, Hanson also composed his first commissioned piece, the string Quartet in One Movement, Opus 23, for the Elizabeth Sprague Coolidge Foundation.

Another work Hanson wrote while in Rome was his Symphony no. 1, Opus 21, the *"Nordic."* In the spring of 1924 he conducted its American premiere in Rochester, New York on the invitation of Albert Coates, who was musical director of the Rochester Philharmonic Orchestra. Here Hanson met Rush Rhees, president of the University of Rochester, and George Eastman, the inventor and founder of Eastman Kodak, whose philanthropy had already been of immense benefit to the University. They were looking for a new head for the Eastman School of Music, and Coates had recommended

Hanson. In conversation with Rhees and Eastman, Hanson discussed his experience that European education too often divided music into scholarly and practical courses of knowledge, each taught at different institutions, and his conviction that a good American music school should provide both. Eastman and Rhees must have been extremely impressed by his ideas, because within a few months they offered him the position of director of the Eastman School of Music. Hanson hesitated about accepting the position; he was not favorably impressed by Rochester, he was reluctant to leave Rome early, and he was worried about the toll such a job would take on his composing and conducting. At least once, later in life, he speculated publicly about the course his life might have taken if he had refused the position. But, he went on to add, his father had become an invalid, and the fact that he was the sole support of both parents had been a crucial factor in his decision. He accepted the offer.[18]

The Eastman School had opened in 1921, after George Eastman had acquired a private music conservatory called the D.K.G. Institute of Musical Art and presented it to the University. The Eastman School's director for its first two years was Alf Klingenberg, the former director of the Institute, and in 1924 it was being run by a one-year interim acting director, Raymond Wilson, a member of the piano faculty. Its composition faculty had originally included Christian Sinding (succeeded a year later by Selim Palmgren); the opera faculty included the conductor and writer Nicolas Slonimsky and the director Rouben Mamoulian (who later directed the original productions of *Porgy and Bess, Oklahoma!, Carousel, Lost in the Stars,* and sixteen Hollywood films) at the beginnings of their American careers. When Eastman and Rhees appointed Hanson to the position, he was twenty-seven years old. He remained the head of the Eastman School for the next forty years, during which time he raised the School (in Slonimsky's words) "from a provincial conservatory to one of the most important musical institutions in America."[19] In a letter written to Rhees before he had been offered the job, Hanson said, "It will take the life of some man to do it. . . . The director of your school will have to breathe fire into a great machine and endow it with his own enthusiasm for a great cause. . . . [A] great thought would have to be borne there, which by its very bigness and idealism would attract to it all those who believe the same things." These were prophetic words.[20]

THE EASTMAN PERIOD

It would be natural to attempt to discuss a man's life and career in chronological order. However, during his tenure at the Eastman

School, the most active years of his career, Howard Hanson pursued so many different activities in so many areas that it would be impossible to give even an inadequate idea of his accomplishments in each area while maintaining chronological order. Therefore this central section is arranged chronologically only within each category of Hanson's activity: as an administrator, as a leader in his field at the national and international level, as a teacher, as a conductor, as an advocate for American music, and as a composer.

Hanson as Administrator

A New Paradigm

Hanson took over the Eastman School at a significant time for American music education. Up to this period, Europe had furnished the model, and a large proportion of the faculty, for American music schools. Most Americans who wanted and could afford a good musical education had travelled to Europe to study in Berlin or Leipzig. (Even after this period, of course, many continued to do so, especially with Nadia Boulanger in Paris.) A shift was occurring, however, in the American attitude toward European models of music education, which can be detected in the contemporaneous founding of the Eastman School of Music and the other two most prestigious conservatories in the country, New York's Juilliard School in 1920 and Philadelphia's Curtis Institute in 1924. Hanson's views on this trend may have been a substantial factor in his being hired by the Eastman School.[21] He toured a number of prominent European music schools, which reinforced his convictions, before he began his job at the Eastman School. Like other American educators, he worked to change the paradigm for his institution from the traditional model of the music conservatory as essentially a group of private studios, each focused narrowly on teaching the mastery of a single musical skill, toward the university model, in which musical training was only a part of a broad educational program.

Hanson embraced the university conception whole-heartedly. He steered the Eastman School toward becoming "a school of music which will graduate students who will be musically well-equipped, in the fields of theory and music history as well as in that of performance, and possessing a general educational background broad enough so that they can, upon that foundation, develop themselves as intelligent, reasoning men and women."[22] When he became director of the School, academic subjects were being taught by teachers on loan from the main campus of the University of Rochester.

Hanson persuaded President Rhees to allow the Eastman School to hire its own academic faculty.

As a result of this change in paradigms, during Hanson's first decade the Eastman School shifted its emphasis from its preparatory and special students (the latter being part-time students who usually took no courses except private lessons in their chosen instrument) to regular college-course students, and from professional certificate programs to college degree programs. When Hanson arrived at the Eastman School, more than half of the students were in certificate programs; by the 1930s, virtually none of them were, and the certificate programs were dropped from the Eastman School catalog. Meanwhile, as student enrollment grew dramatically, the original seven applied music departments—violin, viola, cello, harp, piano, organ, and voice—grew to seventeen, and each of these departments expanded significantly.

Because of the rapid growth in the student population—over one hundred percent in Hanson's first two decades—the School was able to raise its standards for admission and to increase scholarships and awards based both on financial need and on talent. It also rapidly diversified the student body, which changed within Hanson's first decade from approximately 90 percent New York state residents to approximately 30 percent, with a steadily increasing number of foreign students. The number of students transferring from other colleges increased as well, a sign of the School's increased prestige, until transfer students constituted almost half of all new students.

Instrumental and Vocal Performance

It was Hanson's firm conviction that the basis of a student's musical education was the making of music, as either creator or performer. After his arrival, greater emphasis was put on orchestral performance, so that every applied music student belonged to one or more ensembles that performed regularly. In less than a decade, the Eastman student orchestra grew in size from fewer than thirty players, some of whom were faculty, to an all-student ensemble more than one hundred strong. Its quality was considered so high that it became the first student orchestra to present a regular series of broadcasts over a national radio network (NBC) in 1931, which was followed by many radio (and later television) broadcasts on both the CBS and NBC networks. Soon the school established a second full orchestra, then a third, in addition to chamber orchestras and two bands, all of which were often heard on radio. In 1952 the Eastman

Symphonic Wind Ensemble was established under the direction of Frederick Fennell. Eastman graduates went on to leading positions in orchestras everywhere in the United States. With the possible exception of Juilliard, the Eastman School became the most prominent training ground in the country for orchestral musicians.

In addition to orchestral and chamber ensembles, the School also created choral ensembles, the first of which Hanson himself organized and conducted for two years, and a large opera department that specialized in presenting operas in English. In 1955 the Eastman School Collegium Musicum, an ensemble specializing in historically informed performances of early music, was founded, and in 1958 Hanson established the Eastman Philharmonia, an elite orchestra of upperclassmen that, in addition to its concerts around the country, made both broadcasts and recordings. In the winter of 1961–62 the Philharmonia was selected by the State Department to perform on an international tour of cultural exchange. With Hanson conducting, the orchestra played concerts in thirty-four cities and sixteen countries throughout Europe, the Middle East, and Russia, to great acclaim and enthusiastic reviews.

Theory and Musicianship

Believing that many music curricula concentrated unduly on either instrumental skill or musicological research, Hanson put a strong emphasis on ear training and aural skills for all students, including sight-singing, dictation (melodic, harmonic, and rhythmic) and keyboard harmony, which was soon supplemented by training in counterpoint. Research on the pedagogy of aural comprehension in 1950s under Allen Irvine McHose, the chair of the theory department, significantly reduced the numbers of students failing aural skills and theory courses, improved teaching procedures, and led to a number of publications.

Music Education and Research

In his first year, Hanson supervised the affiliation of the Eastman School's music education department with the Rochester public school system, sharing faculty between them. This long-standing close association benefited both the public schools and Eastman's students. He also vastly expanded the holdings of the School's Sibley Music Library, which grew from fewer than ten thousand volumes when he was hired to more than twelve times that amount when he retired, so that it became "the largest collegiate music library for reference and research in the United States."[23]

Graduate Programs

Although he had not gone to graduate school himself, graduate education in music became an important concern of Hanson's. A graduate curriculum was established at the Eastman School in the 1926–27 academic year, and the first doctoral students were accepted in 1931. By the time Hanson retired, graduate students constituted a quarter of the student body. An innovation for which Hanson was largely responsible, and for which he campaigned for two decades, was the establishment of a new performance-oriented doctoral degree, the Doctor of Musical Arts (D.M.A.). Like other educators he felt that the Doctor of Philosophy degree, while appropriate for musicologists and theorists, was not well suited to the needs and goals of many graduate students in music, and the D.M.A. degree recognized doctoral-level artistic achievement, with emphasis on performance and teaching. There was considerable controversy over its eventual adoption and authorization by the National Association of Schools of Music, including an open exchange of letters between Hanson and the musicologist Paul Henry Lang.[24] The Eastman School awarded the first D.M.A. in the United States in 1955, prompting Hanson to write that at last music education had been fully integrated into the academic community, "changing from the European conservatory pattern to the American university pattern," and that "[a]t least we ceased creating bad musicologists out of good violinists, which should prove a boon both to musicology and to violin playing."[25]

Later Criticisms

From all accounts, Hanson proved himself to be an able administrator. After he retired, however, a number of criticisms were heard. One was that he had run the Eastman School as a virtual dictator. Given his position and the length of his tenure, however, it is hard to imagine how he could have run such a large institution effectively without an "iron hand," and the consensus among people who knew him seems to be that he was personally genial and approachable, strong but usually fair, with a sincere interest in and knowledge about Eastman School students. He could, however, be touchy on matters affecting his ego as a composer, and occasionally he would erupt in anger during rehearsals if orchestra players—

either professionals or students—were clowning or giving insufficient respect to the music.

Another criticism heard at the Eastman School and elsewhere was that during his tenure—and for some years afterward—musical scholarship, in the sense of research in musicology and especially music theory, had been neglected in the Eastman School curriculum. To some extent this criticism is unfair; both theory and musicology had had more of a presence in the Eastman School during this period than in the other major conservatories such as Juilliard, Peabody, and Curtis. Still, it is true that Hanson took pride in the fact that Eastman emphasized performance and creation as much as, if not more than, scholarship. He had a jaundiced view of music programs, such as the one at Harvard University, that had traditionally emphasized scholarship at the expense of creativity:

> We equate the creative arts with scholarship. . . . Music means not composers or performers, but historians, theoreticians and music critics. . . . [T]he American universities, and particularly the most conservative of our graduate schools, have pretty well succeeded in sterilizing the creative arts.[26]

While he considered theory and musicology to be important, he saw them from his own viewpoint, as necessary components of a musician's education, rather than as vocations in themselves.

Hanson as Leader in the Musical World

During his time at the Eastman School, Hanson was also actively involved with the field of music education at a national level. At various times he served as president of the Music Teachers National Association, president of the National Association of Schools of Music, and chairman of its Commission on Graduate Study. He served as president of the National Music Council, which he helped to found, for over twenty years. One of his projects in this capacity was to establish a program of residencies for composers in public schools, funded by the Ford Foundation.[27] In 1939 he was also a founding member of the American Music Center, along with Aaron Copland, Otto Luening, Harrison Kerr, Marion Bauer, and Quincy Porter. In the 1960s he was a member of the concert advisory panel of the New York Council of the Arts, the Board of Directors of the Music Educators National Conference, and the advisory committee on the arts of the National Cultural Center, which eventually became the Kennedy Center in Washington, D.C. Among the causes for which he fought over many years, besides the Kennedy Center and the introduction of the Doctor of Musical Arts degree, was the National Endowment for the Arts, which was established in 1965.

Hanson was a strong believer in cultural exchange as a means toward international understanding and amity, and he worked for the arts and cultural cooperation at an international level. From its inception in 1946 he served for many years in a variety of capacities in the U.S. National Commission for UNESCO (the United Nations Educational, Scientific, and Cultural Organization), including chair of the Panel on Music, member of the Program Committee, and long-term member of the executive committee of the International Music Council, which had as its goal "to assist composers in the publication, recording, and dissemination of their works, to bring together composers, educators, and musicologists for the purpose of furthering international understanding."[28] He also served as an advisor to the State Department on cultural exchange for many years.

Among the many honors he received during his career, in 1935 he was elected to the National Institute of Arts and Letters; in 1938, he was named a fellow of Sweden's Royal Academy of Music; in 1950 he was elected to the American Philosophical Society, perhaps the first professional musician to have been admitted to membership in the Society's history; and in 1961 he was elected a member of the American Academy of Arts and Sciences. His awards included the Alice M. Ditson Award in 1945, the Laurel Leaf Award from the American Composers Alliance in 1957, the Huntington Hartford Foundation Award in 1959, and the Medal of Honor from the National Arts Club in 1962.

Hanson as Teacher

As might be expected when a composer was put at the head of a music school, one change that Hanson brought to the Eastman School immediately was a new emphasis on composition, both as a musical activity for all students to practice and as a field of study. Composition became an academic major, and the number of composition majors grew steadily. (Hanson later noted that the 1920s had also shown a dramatic increase in the number of American composers producing concert works, even before he began his own efforts in this area.)[29]

With a prominent composer as its director and a stronger emphasis on composition as an academic major, it was natural that the

Eastman School would become an important training ground for composers as well as instrumentalists. Among the many successful composers who studied at the Eastman School during the Hanson years, although not with Hanson himself, were Thomas Canning, Nathaniel Dett, David Diamond, Samuel Jones, Homer Keller, Gail Kubik, Vladimir Ussachevsky, and Alec Wilder.

Despite his duties as head of the School and his activities outside of it, Hanson continued to teach composition himself. Many of his students later won recognition, including Dominick Argento, Wayne Barlow, Jack Beeson, William Bergsma, Ulysses S. Kay, Kent Kennan, John La Montaine, Peter Mennin, Gardner Read, and Robert Ward. (Argento, La Montaine, and Ward went on to win Pulitzer Prizes in music.)

Hanson also travelled to other schools and institutions as a guest teacher and conductor. In the 1940s, at Serge Koussevitsky's invitation, he taught at the Berkshire Music Center at Tanglewood. Another frequent beneficiary of his industry was the National Music Camp in Interlochen, Michigan. Throughout his life Hanson had close ties with the Camp; he helped to raise funds for it even before it opened its doors in 1928, and he visited during its first summer season. He joined the Board of Directors a few years later, and often guest-conducted the high school orchestra, which he enjoyed greatly.[30]

He made a number of significant forays into teaching by less traditional means as well. Beginning in 1938 he presented, with the Eastman orchestra and other student ensembles, a series of weekly radio programs entitled "Milestones in the History of Music," a survey of the history of Western music, broadcast on local station WHAM and the NBC Red Network. Hanson, the Eastman School and WHAM won the George Foster Peabody Award in 1946 (for outstanding service to music by the broadcasting industry) for this series. During the same period Hanson and the Eastman ensembles presented a similar series on the CBS network entitled "Milestones in American Music," a more-or-less chronological survey that presented orchestral, choral and chamber works by eighty-two American composers from the mid-nineteenth century to the present. It was, in Hanson's words, "the first attempt at a rather complete presentation of the American picture in music."[31] In the 1950s he made a series of television films on composition, sponsored by the Ford Foundation, and in the 1960s he conducted and hosted several series of young people's concerts for Los Angeles schoolchildren with the Los Angeles Philharmonic, which were enthusiastically received.[32] He also made a series of three long-playing

records entitled *The Composer and His Orchestra* for Mercury
Records. Each of these recordings focused on a different aspect of
composition for orchestra; on the first side was a lecture by Hanson,
using excerpts from one of his orchestral works (the *Merry Mount*
Suite, *Mosaics,* or *For the First Time*) to illustrate the subject, and on
the second side, a complete performance of the work.

Hanson's last major pedagogic activity during his time at the
Eastman School was the publication in book form of his theoretical
system. As we shall see in the fourth chapter of this book, where the
chronology of the theory's origin and development will be discussed
in more detail, he had been working on the theory for many years,
and preparing it for publication for a decade, when it finally appeared in the book *Harmonic Materials of Modern Music: Resources of the Tempered Scale*, published by Appleton-Century-Crofts
early in 1960.

Hanson as Conductor

His academic and composing commitments prevented Hanson
from maintaining a truly active career as a conductor during his
years at Eastman. Nevertheless, he often made guest appearances
with the Rochester Philharmonic Orchestra. He also continued to
guest-conduct other orchestras three or four times a year. At one
time or another he conducted virtually every symphony orchestra in
the country—most often the Boston Symphony, the Los Angeles
Philharmonic, the New York Philharmonic, the National Symphony, the NBC Symphony (and its post-Toscanini incarnation, the
Symphony of the Air), and the San Francisco Symphony. In the
early 1930s he also conducted concerts of American music with the
Berlin Philharmonic, the Berlin Radio Symphony, and orchestras
in Leipzig and Stuttgart. In addition, he acted as guest conductor
with many university orchestras and bands through the years.

Hanson had no training at all in conducting, as he was the first
to admit. Perhaps as a result, his baton technique seems to have been
somewhat faulty; musicians who played under him remember that
his beat tended to be circular rather than definite. Despite this, he
was considered a very good conductor. Like other conductors with
technical limitations such as Wilhelm Furtwängler, he managed to
get across what he wanted effectively, and he was considered particularly powerful at communicating emotion to and through his orchestras. Many students and colleagues have also testified to his
ability to sight-read and play a new orchestral score at the piano
with uncanny accuracy.[33]

Hanson as Champion of American Music

Performances

When he was appointed to the directorship of the Eastman School in 1924, Hanson decided that one of the School's goals should be the fostering and promotion of American music, both new and old. In 1925, he founded the quarterly American Composers' Concerts at the Eastman School, "a laboratory for composers, a place where the young composer might come and hear his works performed by a competent orchestra."[34] Using the Rochester Philharmonic Orchestra and the facilities of the Eastman School, Hanson was able to give each of the selected works not only a performance, but a fully finished performance by a fine orchestra, rehearsed in the presence of the composers, whose travel and living expenses had been paid, as well as the costs of copying parts.[35] In fact every concert but the very first one represented two performances, because all subsequent programs were repeated after an intermission. This was an opportunity without parallel, either then or now, for young American composers. As Hanson put it several years later, "In the American Concerts it is not necessary for the composer to have a box-office reputation. We are, in fact, more interested in discovering worthwhile new talent than in re-performing works of established artists."[36] The first concert in May 1925, selected by a jury consisting of Ernest Bloch, Albert Coates, and Hanson, included pieces by Bernard Rogers, Quincy Porter, and Aaron Copland. (The Copland piece was the world premiere of *Cortège Macabre*, an excerpt salvaged from his ballet *Grohg*. This was only the second performance anywhere of an orchestral work by Copland. *Grohg* was never performed during Copland's lifetime, although he later used some other excerpts in the *Dance Symphony*.)[37]

Hanson, who conducted the Concerts without a fee, continued to supervise the selection of works every year, attempting to ensure that the stylistic range of works chosen was as wide as possible. Characteristically, he would announce publicly "that some of the numbers which we played I cordially disliked, though I would do my best to keep the audience from discovering which they were!"[38] In 1935 the School began making archival recordings of the Concerts, and in 1936 the Concerts were supplemented by the Symposia of American Music: a fall Symposium with readings of new works, in all genres, from composers across the country, and a spring Symposium with readings of works by Eastman School students. Both Symposia used a more informal and less official format, with Hanson usually conducting in shirtsleeves, and both were often

featured in radio broadcasts. Such opportunities for student composers were, again, virtually unprecedented.

Meanwhile in 1931, on the tenth anniversary of the founding of
the Eastman School of Music, Hanson had instituted the Festival of
American Music, an annual event that eventually became a week-
long series of concerts featuring both premieres of new works and
repeat performances of older works, including those of more established American composers. In addition to the concerts of orchestral
music, which continued to bear the title of American Composers'
Concerts, the Festivals eventually included chamber music, band
and wind ensemble music, vocal and choral music, opera, and ballet, many with student performers. As with the American Composers' Concerts and the Symposia, excerpts from the Festival programs—and sometimes complete programs—were for years regularly broadcast over national radio networks. Olin Downes, chief
music critic of the *New York Times*, came away from the first Festival "greatly impressed" by what he saw of young composers
"working with immense enthusiasm and with the intention of un-
sparing self-criticism," and feeling that nowhere else in the country was there "such a vigorous, healthy and productive spirit."[39] The
Festivals were instrumental in reviving the works of American
composers whose music had already been forgotten, such as George
W. Chadwick, Arthur Foote, John Knowles Paine, and Horatio
Parker. With all of this activity Rochester grew from a small
industrial city into one that was, for the rest of Hanson's lifetime at
least, a national center of musical activity, and one that was extremely supportive of the Eastman School's activities. The Festival
performances, which were free to the public, had consistently full
houses even in the three-thousand-seat Eastman Theatre, and ticket
seekers were often turned away.

The Festivals of American Music continued under Hanson's
direction until 1971, seven years after his retirement from the
Eastman School. Thanks to the resources and facilities of the
University of Rochester, Hanson had been able to continue both the
Festivals and the Symposia even through the years of the Great
Depression and World War II, when other such ventures foundered.
During the forty-six years of these concerts, Hanson presented thou-
sands of works by hundreds of American composers. Among the
many who had orchestral and chamber pieces premiered (and often
repeated) at the American Composers' Concerts or the Festivals of
American Music were Dominick Argento, Ernst Bacon, Wayne
Barlow, Robert Russell Bennett, William Bergsma, Thomas Can-
ning, Elliott Carter, Aaron Copland, Henry Cowell, Paul Creston,
Nathaniel Dett, David Diamond, Vittorio Giannini, Charles Tom-

linson Griffes, Roy Harris, Alan Hovhaness, Ulysses S. Kay, Kent Kennan, Leo Kraft, Gail Kubik, John La Montaine, Otto Luening, Colin McPhee, Peter Mennin, Douglas Moore, Vincent Persichetti, Quincy Porter, Gardner Read, Wallingford Riegger, Bernard Rogers, Ned Rorem, Elie Siegmeister, Leo Sowerby, Robert Starer, William Grant Still, Randall Thompson, and Robert Ward. It has been said more than once of the Festivals that "more native music has been played at these concerts than in all the rest of the United States put together."[40]

In the Festival programs Hanson attempted "to maintain the broadest catholicity of taste in the selection of the works performed to include everything from the experimentalists of their day to the conservatives," with the goal of presenting "a cross-section of the creative musical history of the United States."[41] Indeed, unlike many other musicians who have been in similar positions, Hanson was generally acknowledged not to have let his own stylistic predilections influence unduly his choice of music to be performed.[42] There is currently a general impression, shared by people who were at the Eastman School in the late 1950s and 1960s, that by that time the stylistic range of the concerts had become narrower.[43] Yet the programs of the concerts refute this. Although few, if any, twelve-tone or aleatory works were programmed in later years, there had been none at all in earlier years; while on the other hand, contemporary works of jazz, Latin American, and electronic music (by such composers as Edgard Varèse, Karlheinz Stockhausen, and Vladimir Ussachevsky) were featured on a number of concerts in this period, and Hanson continued to program such "modernist" composers as Henry Cowell and Wallingford Riegger. He also continued to demand respect for composers whose work, regardless of its style, showed solid technique and craftmanship. During the rehearsal of an *avant-garde* piece for an American Composers' Concert in 1962 that was going poorly, Hanson, hearing resentment in the orchestra against the music, stopped the rehearsal and asked one of the bass players if he disliked the piece. The player said yes. Hanson asked several more players, including the concertmaster, and all agreed that they disliked the piece. Hanson replied that he didn't much like the piece either, but that the composer had written it, that it was well-crafted and had integrity, and that they were going to perform it. Anyone who did not want to play it, he added angrily, could "get the hell out of here!"[44]

It is true that as time went on the concerts included more music from previous concerts and less new music, but this was intentional. It was Hanson's conviction that a musical work, in order to have a chance of entering the repertory, needed not a single performance but a number of performances. Thus the student Symposia gradually replaced the American Composers' Concerts as the "experimental laboratory" for new works. It is also true that after 1951 the fall Symposium was replaced by a single American Composers' Concert, and that the proportion of music by Eastman faculty and alumni in the concerts, especially the Symposia and the nonorchestral concerts, increased over the years; but during the same period the composition program at the Eastman School had grown considerably, and Hanson seems to have felt that his first responsibility was to the increased numbers of his own student and faculty composers.[45]

Publications

In 1926 Hanson began a collateral project of publishing new American musical scores from among those works performed at the American Composers' Concerts. By the time he retired, forty scores had been published in this series—of which nine were by Hanson and many of the rest by Eastman School faculty and students—as well as a number of textbooks. When the publication budget was drastically cut during the Great Depression, he assigned half of his copyrights to the Eastman School, stipulating that the royalties from those works be used to fund the publication project.[46]

New Media

Hanson saw recordings and broadcasting as further ways to help promote American music, providing more chances for new works to become known and accepted. In 1939 he created the Eastman-Rochester (or Eastman-Rochester Symphony) Orchestra, which was an *ad hoc* ensemble comprised of players from the Rochester Philharmonic and the Eastman School faculty, supplemented by students and community players. With this orchestra, between 1939 and 1969, Hanson made over one hundred recordings for 78-rpm and long-playing black-vinyl discs, first for RCA Victor and later for Mercury Records, as well as a handful for Columbia Records. These recordings consisted in large part of works from the American Composers' Concerts and the Festivals of American Music. (According to one source, Hanson took no royalties for any of his own compositions on these recordings.)[47]

The Eastman-Rochester Orchestra was neither a permanent institution nor as large as more famous orchestras, and occasionally its recordings were criticized for a rather dry acoustic or an undersized string tone compared to those of first-rank orchestras. Nevertheless, as mentioned above, these recordings were and continue to be highly regarded, and many of them have been rereleased on compact disc. As a 1962 review put it, "Howard Hanson has made more and better records of modern American music than anybody else alive," and twenty years later his recordings were called "benchmarks for younger conductors who wish to interpret the American repertoire."[48] (The Eastman-Rochester Orchestra should not be confused either with the Eastman School student orchestras or with the Rochester Philharmonic Orchestra, a professional orchestra that included members of the Eastman School faculty. The Rochester Philharmonic was an autonomous organization, and Hanson was never its regular conductor.[49] The same is true of the Rochester Civic Orchestra, the core group of the Rochester Philharmonic, which often performed as a chamber orchestra.)

Public Speaking and Writing

During and after the Eastman School years, in addition to all of the above activities, Hanson gave numerous addresses and speeches—at concerts, lecture series, club meetings and awards ceremonies, regional and national conferences and conventions, church services and congressional committees, dedications, luncheons and dinners, symposia and informal talks, commencements and convocations, festivals and world's fairs, pre-concert lectures, and radio and television broadcasts—most often on topics related to music education, or "lectures which were quite frankly propaganda for American music."[50] He also contributed four or five articles a year to music journals and national magazines.[51] The texts of his speeches reveal an articulate and forceful mind, commanding a wide range of knowledge in many areas of expertise, marshalling persuasive evidence to illustrate his convictions, and constantly leavening his serious points with wry and often self-deprecating wit. According to people who heard him, Hanson was a powerfully eloquent speaker, capable of moving an audience to both laughter and tears.

Summary

Of the many testimonials to Hanson's importance in the cause of promoting American music, only a few more will be cited here. In Hanson's obituary in The New York Times Harold C. Schonberg wrote, "It is safe to say that nearly every American composer after

World War I was in his debt to some degree." According to Joseph Machlis, "Howard Hanson's achievement extends beyond his activities as a composer. It may safely be said that in the second quarter of the twentieth century no individual . . . did more for the cause of American music than he." And in the words of William Grant Still—whose *Afro-American Symphony* and other works were premiered by Hanson and who, like other African-American composers, found in Hanson an early supporter—"Dr. Hanson has done more, perhaps, than anyone in the United States for the music of this country."[52]

Hanson as Composer

Despite the drain on his time and energy imposed by his other activities, Hanson continued an active career as a composer. While he was not extremely prolific, he continued to produce an average of eight substantial works during each decade of his tenure at the Eastman School, most of them commissioned by such sources as the CBS radio network, UNESCO, the symphony orchestras of New York, Boston, Cleveland, and Cincinnati, and many colleges and universities.

This output included four symphonies, numbers 2 through 5. The Symphony no. 2, Opus 30, subtitled by Hanson the *"Romantic,"* was commissioned by Serge Koussevitsky for the fiftieth anniversary of the Boston Symphony Orchestra (along with such works as Stravinsky's *Symphony of Psalms*). It was a conscious gesture of defiance against the anti-Romantic spirit of the times. As Hanson wrote at the time, "Much contemporary music seems to me to be showing a tendency to become entirely too cerebral. I do not believe that music is primarily a matter of the intellect, but rather a manifestation of the emotions. I have therefore aimed in this symphony to create a work that was young in spirit, lyrical and romantic in temperament, and simple and direct in expression."[53] Since its premiere in 1930 it has remained Hanson's most popular and often-performed major work. Its lyrical, haunting second theme has been quoted in many places and contexts, and often—perhaps too often—by Hanson himself.[54] At the National Music Camp in Interlochen, Michigan it became the "Interlochen theme," played at the end of every orchestra concert, and as such it has become indelibly associated in the minds of several generations of musicians with memories of lovely evenings in the northern woods. One of the more incongruous uses to which this theme has been subjected was as the music heard over the closing credits of the horror movie *Alien* in 1979. (Hanson was not consulted by his publisher on the granting of rights for this use, and when he found out about it after the movie opened, he was extremely angry. Eventually he decided that it was not worth trying to fight.)[55]

The Symphony no. 3, Opus 33, written "in commemoration of the 300th anniversary of the first Swedish settlement on the shores of Delaware," was commissioned by the CBS radio network. Hanson conducted the first three movements on a CBS broadcast in 1937, although he first conducted the complete symphony with the NBC Symphony Orchestra in 1938. (Hanson was the first native-born American to conduct the NBC Symphony, which had been created for Arturo Toscanini.) Serge Koussevitsky was a particular champion of this symphony; in 1939 he called it the finest American symphony that had yet been written, "the equal of any of the great symphonies."[56] Hanson's Symphony no. 4, Opus 34, subtitled *Requiem* (in memory of his father), which was premiered by the Boston Symphony Orchestra under Hanson's baton, won the second Pulitzer Prize for music in 1944.[57] His *Sinfonia Sacra* (Symphony no. 5), Opus 43, was premiered by the Philadelphia Orchestra under Eugene Ormandy in 1955.

Another work written during the Eastman years was Hanson's only opera, *Merry Mount*, one of the small number of American operas commissioned by New York's Metropolitan Opera Company. *Merry Mount*, with a libretto by Richard L. Stokes, was based loosely upon Nathaniel Hawthorne's short story "The Maypole of Merry Mount," and thus had not only an American composer and librettist but an American source and an American subject.[58] Unlike most other Metropolitan Opera commissions, *Merry Mount* was accepted for performance before the score had even been written.[59] The Metropolitan premiere in February 1934, which starred Lawrence Tibbett and was conducted by Tullio Serafin, was broadcast nationally on radio. At this premiere, which was accompanied by a blizzard of press coverage and discussion, a wildly enthusiastic audience gave the cast and the creators fifty curtain calls. Nine performances followed in its first season. The reviews, however, while generally positive, were mixed—only the choruses being universally praised—and when general manager Giulio Gatti-Cassazza left shortly afterward, *Merry Mount,* and all other American works, disappeared from the Metropolitan stage. Since then, *Merry Mount* has had relatively few professional productions, most likely because of the unappealing character of its Puritan protagonist and other limitations of Stokes's libretto, and because Hanson sometimes allowed musical considerations to outweigh dramatic ones, as he himself later acknowledged.[60] Nevertheless, the Suite that Hanson drew from his music for the opera remains one of his most

popular pieces. Years later he said he was interested in writing another opera, but had had problems finding a suitable libretto.[61]

Other major works from this period include *The Lament for
Beowulf*, Opus 25, for chorus and orchestra, which was written
shortly after his return from Rome; the Concerto for Piano and
Orchestra, Opus 36, which was first performed in 1948 by Rudolf
Firkusny with Hanson conducting the Boston Symphony Orchestra;
the *Elegy*, Opus 44, written in memory of Serge Koussevitsky and
premiered in 1956 by the Boston Symphony under Charles Munch;
Mosaics, a theme-and-variations written for and premiered by
George Szell and the Cleveland Orchestra in 1958; a number of
highly regarded works for band, including the *Chorale and
Alleluia*; and the two concertante chamber pieces that Hanson wrote
as gifts for his wife—the *Serenade for Flute, Harp, and Strings*,
Opus 35, first performed by Georges Laurent and the Boston
Symphony under Koussevitsky in 1945, and the *Pastorale for Oboe,
Strings, and Harp* (originally for oboe and piano), Opus 38, first per-
formed in its orchestral version by Marcel Tabuteau and the
Philadelphia Orchestra under Eugene Ormandy in 1950. Hanson
also wrote a considerable number of works for chorus and orchestra
(often to texts by Walt Whitman), such as *Songs from "Drum Taps,"
The Cherubic Hymn*, and the *Song of Democracy*.[62]

While many details of Hanson's compositional methods will be
discussed in the analytical chapters of this book, a brief summary of
characteristic elements of his music may be useful for those who are
unfamiliar with it—notwithstanding the many grains of salt that
must be taken with this, as with any generalized discussion of a
composer's style. It would not be inaccurate to consider Hanson as
essentially a Romantic, although his Romanticism is unquestionably twentieth-century in its sound. (It should also be pointed out that
until Hanson declared his allegiance with the "Romantic" Symphony in 1930, he was considered a modernist.)[63] Like much of Aaron
Copland's music, and for some of the same technical reasons, much
of his music sounds "rugged," "vigorous," and "American" to many
listeners, often suggesting the open spaces of the West. Hanson
himself said, "My music springs from the soil of the American
mid-West. It is music of the plains rather than of the city and reflects, I believe, something of the broad prairies of my native
Nebraska."[64] Grounded in tradition, the harmonic practice of his
maturity could be described as expanded tonality or "pantonality"—
tonal centricity without the consistent use of functional progressions, major or minor mode, or traditional triadic structures—although it often makes use of triads and often implies the major or
minor mode. Some of the stylistic "fingerprints" that can be found

throughout many of his works are passages based on modal scales, especially the Dorian; themes derived from or reminiscent of Lutheran chorales or Gregorian chant; extended tertian chords such as sevenths, ninths, elevenths, and thirteenths; quartal and quintal harmonies; pedal points (late in life, Hanson said that he might have been overaddicted to pedal points); motoric ostinati in fast passages; and a back-and-forth alternation between two triads or altered triadic chords, often over a dissonant pedal. Instrumental fingerprints in Hanson's orchestral pieces include the use of the piccolo in its highest registers, even more extensive (and more shrill) than in Mahler; a galloping long-short, long-short rhythm on the snare drum in fast passages, usually underneath a jagged melody in the xylophone and high woodwinds; and (especially in the earlier pieces) lush strings, either subdivided into chords or singing a lyric melody in parallel octaves.

In addition to these general stylistic traits of Hanson's, there are also many cases where passages in different pieces from the same period resemble each other. For instance, there are strong resemblances among the love theme from *Merry Mount*, the main theme of the second movement of the First Symphony, and the second theme of the Second Symphony; between the fast passages in *The Mystic Trumpeter* and the second movement of the Sixth Symphony; and among the main themes of the first and second movements of the Piano Concerto, the third movement of the Symphony no. 4, and the fast section of the *Pastorale for Oboe, Strings, and Harp*. Such resemblances, of course, may be found among the works of many composers with distinctive musical personalities, and do not necessarily show that Hanson had a limited tonal palette. Whatever his other limitations as a composer may have been, later chapters of this book will make clear that the common conception of Hanson's style—based primarily upon two or three of his best-known pieces, the first two symphonies and the *Merry Mount* Suite, all written before 1935—does him an injustice. His style was neither uniform nor unchanging. In fact, these works are representative neither of the styles of other early pieces nor of his later style, which in general could be called leaner, more compressed or granitic, and less lyrical or rhapsodic. It is true that, unlike the styles of many twentieth-century composers, Hanson's overall style changed by a slow and very gradual evolution, not an abrupt *volte-face*; but those who are familiar with only the three best-known pieces, and do not know such early works as *Lux Aeterna, The Lament for Beowulf,* and *Pan and the Priest,* or such later works as the *Serenade for Flute, Harp and Strings, The Cherubic Hymn,* and the Symphony no. 6, have little idea of Hanson's range.[65]

PRIVATE LIFE AND RETIREMENT

After forty-nine years as a bachelor, in 1946 Hanson married Margaret E. Nelson of Chautauqua, New York, a lakeside resort town about one hundred miles southwest of Rochester. An amateur singer and musician herself, she was almost twenty years younger than he. As he later told the story, while she was thinking over his marriage proposal, he wrote the *Serenade for Flute, Harp, and Strings* and sent her a recording as a Christmas present, in the hope that it would help plead his cause—and it worked. To all appearances they were a happy and almost inseparable couple, and she accompanied him on virtually all of his travels and concert tours.[66] They had no children. In an interview at the age of seventy, Hanson speculated that if he had not taken the Eastman position, and had remained an independent composer or a teacher rather than an administrator, he might well have married earlier and had children, although he appeared to be content with the way his life had gone. He seemed to feel that as partial compensation he had had personal or collegial relationships with many of the thousands of students who had gone through the Eastman School during his time there.[67]

In the early 1960s, Hanson began to talk publicly about his intention to retire from the directorship of the Eastman School, and the discussion of a retirement date and a possible successor continued for several years. He did finally retire in the spring of 1964, at the age of sixty-seven. His successor as director of the Eastman School was the conductor Walter Hendl.

Even then, however, Hanson remained almost as busy as he had been before. His compositional output increased, though not dramatically. It included his Symphony no. 6, a six-movement work commissioned by the New York Philharmonic for its 125th anniversary, and premiered by the Philharmonic in 1968 with Hanson conducting; *Dies Natalis*, a set of variations on a chorale theme for orchestra (or band); the suite for wind ensemble and piano solo called *Young Person's Guide to the Six-Tone Scale*; his choral Symphony no. 7, *A Sea Symphony*, to texts by Walt Whitman, written for the 50th anniversary of the National Music Camp and premiered there by the eighty-year-old composer in a concert of his works in 1977;[68] a number of other major pieces for chorus and orchestra, including *The Mystic Trumpeter*, *Lumen in Christo*, and *New Land, New Covenant*; and Hanson's last completed work, the ballet suite for chamber orchestra entitled *Nymph and Satyr*.

In addition to composing, Hanson continued to conduct, write, and speak, and to serve on boards, committees, and juries. He also took on new responsibilities. In 1965 he became editor-in-chief of the

Scribner Music Library, a series of twelve volumes of pieces for piano students. (Originally he planned to collaborate with Nicolas
Slonimsky on a volume on music history and theory for the
Scribner Music Library, for which Slonimsky would write the historical portion and Hanson the theoretical portion, including a section dealing with his theory of chromatic relations. This volume
never appeared.)[69] From 1966 to 1976 he wrote a biweekly series of
articles on music and related topics for the *Rochester Times-Union,*
one of the two leading newspapers in the area; he served as vice-
president and honorary board chairman of a local ballet company;
and after twenty years as president of the National Music Council,
he retired from the position and was named chairman of the board.

When Hanson retired from the Eastman School, the University
of Rochester created a new entity called the Institute of American
Music, with Hanson as its first director, to continue his efforts in
promoting, performing and recording American music. The Institute took over part of the sponsorship of the Festivals and Symposia of
American Music, and Hanson continued to select the material and
conduct the concerts until he retired from this task in 1971, when the
entire enterprise ceased. The Institute also reissued, under the
Eastman-Rochester Archives label, recordings from the American
music series that Hanson had begun with Mercury Records. It was
not simply a so-called "golden parachute" for Hanson: he himself
helped to fund the Institute with royalties, and in 1976 he gave the
Institute $100,000 worth of Kodak stock. (Much of this came from the
money he had inherited from his uncle the actor.)[70] Shortly after the
Institute began he had written, "I have gladly accepted this assignment for my remaining years," and he remained its director
for the rest of his life, although because of changes at the Eastman
School he became increasingly isolated from the Institute's day-to-
day activities, and he was disappointed by decisions taken by the
board in regard to its tax-exempt status, expenditures, marketing,
and new initiatives.[71]

In 1979 Hanson was elected to the American Academy and
Institute of Arts and Letters. He and his wife continued to spend
most of each year at their home in a suburb of Rochester, and divided
their summers among Mrs. Hanson's family home on Lake
Chautauqua, the National Music Camp at Interlochen, and their
house on Bold Island, off the coast of Maine, which Hanson had inherited from his uncle. This house had neither electricity nor running water, and their gas-powered marine telephone worked only
when they wanted it to work. Here with only his wife, their dogs, and
a few selected visitors for company, Hanson composed, swam every
day, chopped wood, and did repair work and various projects with

his hands, until the summer before he died, when he had become too feeble. He died in Rochester on February 26, 1981, at the age of eighty-four. A recital hall, an interfaith chapel and a scholarship continue to bear his name at the Eastman School of Music.

One last aspect of Hanson's career needs to be mentioned at this point, albeit briefly: the precipitous decline of his reputation as a composer, in terms of both critical opinion and general public awareness. This decline began sometime in the late 1950s or early 1960s, and continued with little abatement until several years after his death. Up to this time Hanson had remained prominent, not only as an educator and conductor, but as a composer. Critical opinion of his works had never been universally positive, but as his many awards (including the Pulitzer Prize) show, in the 1940s and 1950s he was generally thought of as one of the most important, if not most radical, of American composers.[72] With his retirement from the Eastman School, however, his name seemed virtually to vanish from discussions of American composers in print.

This change in critical opinion can be ascribed in large part to the vogue for atonal idioms that arose in musical circles after World War II. While the full ramifications of this subject lie beyond the scope of this book, it can be said with some degree of accuracy that there was a major change in the styles of many composers, especially Americans, in the decades following the death of Arnold Schoenberg in 1951 and the subsequent conversion of Igor Stravinsky, the most influential composer of the time, to twelve-tone serial composition. A wave of American composers young and old followed in Stravinsky's path, or similar ones: away from tonality and toward post-Webernian total serialism, aleatory music, *musique concrète*, electronic music, collage, or various free atonal styles. The weight of critical opinion shifted, as young composers and theorists sympathetic to "advanced" styles and aesthetics, and scornful of traditional ones, began to fill the music departments of colleges and universities across the country. Not only Romanticism, but music with any sort of tonal centricity came to be regarded as tired and *passé*.[73]

During this same period, many of the older conductors who had championed Hanson, such as Koussevitsky, Ormandy, and Szell, retired or died; and as daily newspapers merged or went out of business, there were fewer journalists reviewing serious music, so that the young modernists in the academy began to exert proportionately more influence in the field. It was also the first time that more than a few music theorists were undertaking serious attempts to analyze music beyond that of the so-called common-practice period—especially atonal and serial music—and during this time a number of theory journals that were explicitly oriented toward the study of atonal music, such as *Perspectives of New Music* and *Journal of Music Theory,* were founded. Like Samuel Barber, another prominent American Romantic composer, Hanson was now perceived, and usually mentioned, as outdated and overrated.[74] Only Aaron Copland was generally able to escape this slump in critical estimation, thanks not only to his being the most popular of American "classical" composers but also to his attempts to join the *avant-garde* bandwagon and write serially, in comparatively unsuccessful pieces such as *Connotations* and *Inscape.* It was a time—not just in music but in many of the arts—when the rationale behind an artwork was often considered to be more important than the artwork itself. As Copland himself described this trend, "Too often you get the feeling, when you read an analysis, that there isn't much point to the music except the way the darn thing's put together."[75] Perhaps not coincidentally, during this time the audiences for new music became smaller and scarcer.

It was toward the end of this period that Hanson died, already half-forgotten, not only among the music-loving public but among professional musicians as well. A sad indicator of the decline in his critical stature by the time of his death appeared in *The New York Times* in the form of a column that accompanied his obituary, written by a *Times* music critic and titled, rather ironically, "An Appreciation." While condescendingly allowing that some of Hanson's music might "warrant occasional revival and reassessment," the writer asserted rather snidely that Hanson's music "strongly suggests a lost world of antimaccasars [*sic*] and stereopticons."[76] Such a comment is, at the very least, inaccurate and misleading, since antimacassars and stereopticons went out of date while Hanson was a child. As though to add insult to injury, the obituary itself (by the *Times*'s chief music critic), although more respectful, incorrectly identified Hanson's most popular piece, the *"Romantic" Symphony*, as his Symphony no. 3.[77] Similarly, Hanson's obituary in *Time* announced that he had "fought tirelessly, if unsuccessfully, against progressive trends in American classical music," which is thoroughly inaccurate in its implication that Hanson actively crusaded to turn back the clock of musical "progress."[78] Another sign of Hanson's critical eclipse is that for several decades, from the early 1970s to the late 1980s, the recordings of his music (besides Eastman School reissues of his own recordings) were few and far between.

Although he did not live to see it, however, shortly after his death the tide began to turn again. Composers began to miss the audiences that had been driven away by their atonal, serial or aleatory works.

A new style called "neo-Romanticism" arose, and essentially Romantic composers such as David Del Tredici and Stephen Albert became prominent and were taken seriously. It was again respectable for composers and theorists to say that the resources of tonal music had not been exhausted (which composers like Hanson—not to mention the public at large—had already known).[79] In the late 1980s, younger conductors such as Leonard Slatkin and Gerard Schwarz began to record Hanson's major pieces, to renewed critical acclaim. Now much of his music is again available in the most current audio format—although few of the major works beyond the Symphony no. 2 have yet to be programmed with any regularity by orchestras. Nevertheless, as with Barber and other American Romantics such as Paul Creston, David Diamond and Robert Ward, Hanson's star has definitely been back in the ascendant during the last decade. A recent column in a magazine that reviews classical recordings quotes "a gleeful staff member at the Music Division of the Library of Congress" as saying, "Finally it's OK to like Howard Hanson again!"[80]

Chapter 3

A Summary of *Harmonic Materials of Modern Music*

Having surveyed Hanson's life and career, we may now survey his theory. In order to discuss and evaluate the theory, however, it will be necessary first to present it. Inasmuch as *Harmonic Materials* is still almost completely unknown, even to music theorists, it will be useful to present a précis of the book, chapter by chapter.[81]

Hanson uses terms throughout his book in ways that few others, except some of his students and their students in turn, have adopted. Throughout this and subsequent chapters Hanson's terminology will necessarily be used, but equivalent terms from set theory will be added for clarity when appropriate, as will illustrative examples and additional comments. In the list below are some of Hanson's most important terms, followed by their commonly accepted equivalents in set theory.[82]

Hanson term	*set-theory term*
tone	pitch class (pc)
sonority or **scale**	pc set or set class (sc)
triad, tetrad, etc.	trichord, tetrachord, etc.
involution	symmetrical set inversion
interval	interval class (ic)
interval analysis	interval vector
isomeric	Z-related
isometric	inversionally symmetrical

Preface

Hanson attributes the impetus for the book to his experience as a composition teacher: "It has developed in an effort to aid gifted young composers . . . searching for an expressive vocabulary." The scope of the book is delimited to "the study of the relationship of tones in melody or harmony without reference to . . . rhythm." Hanson states firmly that it is neither a "method" nor a "system" of composition, but "a compendium of harmonic-melodic material. . . . I hope that this volume may serve the composer in much the same way that a dictionary or thesaurus serves the author." While musical sounds cannot be defined as words can, "it is possible to explain the derivation of a sonority, to analyze its component parts, and describe its position in the tonal cosmos" (pp. viii–xi).

Hanson points out that traditional theory is concerned with only a small fraction of all the possibilities of the chromatic scale—primarily major and minor scales and chords constructed of thirds plus chromatic alterations, which leaves out many of the possibilities of equal-tempered music, including much twentieth-century music. His book attempts to analyze all tonal possibilities inherent in the chromatic scale.

Hanson's scheme of classification uses four main concepts: "interval analysis," including the reduction of all intervals to six basic categories or classes; "projection," which he defines as "the construction of scales or chords by any logical and consistent process of addition and repetition"; "involution," the symmetrical "mirror" inversion of an interval, a group of intervals or a sonority—so named because Hanson wants to avoid confusion with the traditional connotations of "inversion" of tertian chords; and "complementary scales," the complement of a scale consisting of all the tones not contained within that scale. According to Hanson, the latter is perhaps the most important concept in the book, for "it sets up a basis for the logical expansion of tonal ideas once the germinating concept has been decided upon" (p. xi).

While he has written the book for composers, he adds that colleagues think his book can be useful as a guide to analysis of twentieth-century music, with which the theorist can "analyze factually any passage or phrase written in the twelve-tone equally tempered scale" (p. xi).

Chapter 1

The first three chapters serve as introductions to Hanson's system of classification. He begins by explaining the practical reasons for restricting himself to the equal-tempered chromatic scale. He uses the term "sonority" for any collection of tones, presented either linearly or simultaneously. He makes no practical distinction between the melodic or harmonic arrangement of notes of a sonority; "the same effect of dissonance persists in our aural memory if the tones are sounded consecutively." He considers the most important aspect of the sound of a sonority to be the relative consonance or dissonance of its constituents, and considers placement, positioning, doubling, timbre, and historical context to be of comparatively minor importance.

Chapter 2

Hanson makes certain assumptions for interval analysis. He ignores all doubling of pitches; he takes all compound intervals as equivalent to their simple counterparts, all enharmonically related intervals as equivalent to each other, and all intervals as equivalent to their inversions, using a single term for each. "This is not meant to imply that the interval and its inversion are the same, but rather that they perform the same function in a sonority" (p. 9). He uses the symbol p to represent the perfect fourth or fifth (equivalent to set theory's interval class 5, representing five—or seven—semitones), m the major third or minor sixth (equivalent to interval class 4), n the minor third or major sixth (interval class 3)—all of which he says represent intervals that are "commonly considered consonant"; s the major second or minor seventh (ic 2), d the minor second or major seventh (ic 1), and t the tritone (ic 6)—all "considered dissonant." He gives examples of his interval analysis, using numerical superscripts to denote the number of occurrences of each interval in a sonority. For example, the collection of three pitches C-D♭-D, with two minor seconds (between C and D♭ and between D♭ and D) and one major second (between C and D), would be analyzed as sd^2. (The equivalent of this sonority in set theory is [012], with interval vector 210000.[83] In Allen Forte's commonly accepted terminology of set-class names, this is set class 3-1, or sc 3-1.)

Chapter 3

"Every sonority in music has a counterpart obtained by taking the *inverse ratio* of the original sonority" (p. 17). Hanson calls this "projection *down* from the lowest tone of a given chord" the *involution* of that chord. (Sonorities are commonly listed in ascending order. For example, the sonority C-E-F can be considered as a succes-

sion of semitones, four semitones upward from C to E and one
semitone up from E to F. If this succession is taken *downward* from
C, we get C-A♭-G, i.e., four semitones downward from C to A♭ and one
semitone down from A♭ to G. This new sonority, whether listed in
ascending order as G-A♭-C, or in any other order, is the involution of
the original, which is equivalent to the symmetrical or "mirror" inversion of set theory.) Hanson notes that a sonority and its involution always have the same interval analysis. He distinguishes
three types of involution: simple, isometric, and enharmonic. A
simple involution "differs in sound" from the original chord. For
example, the involution of the major triad C-E-G (in which the intervals upward, starting from C, are four and then three semitones)
is C-A♭-F (in which the intervals downward from C are four and
then three semitones) or, put into ascending order, the minor triad
F-A♭-C. An isometric involution has "the same *kind* of sound" as the
original, i.e., is a transposition of the original by any interval other
than one or more octaves. For example, the involution of C-E-G-B is
(going downward from C) C-A♭-F-D♭, or in ascending order, D♭-F-
A♭-C. An enharmonic involution contains "the same tones in different octaves" as the original sonority; for example, the involution
of C-E♭-G♭-A is C-A-G♭-E♭, or in ascending order, C-E♭-G♭-A. All
combinations of sonorities and their involutions are isometric (inversionally symmetrical) sonorities: "they will have the same order of intervals whether considered 'up' or 'down'."

Hanson notes the existence of, and defines as *isomeric*, sonorities that "have the same components but which are not involutions
one of the other"—i.e., which have the same total interval content
(interval vector) but not the same ordering of intervals from each
tone to the next higher one. Isomeric sonorities are thus equivalent
to set theory's Z-related set classes.[84] (Hanson apparently adopts the
term "isomeric" from chemistry, wherein isomers are different
chemical compounds with the same chemical formula.)

Part I: The Six Basic Tonal Series

Chapter 4

Most combinations of tones tend to group themselves into sounds
with a preponderance of one of the six basic intervals. A smaller
number have two basic intervals predominating, some have three,
and a few, which Hanson considers neutral in "color," have four.

Among six-tone sonorities, twenty-six have one predominant interval, twelve have two, six have three and six have four. "The simplest and most direct study of the relationship of tones is, therefore, in terms of the projection of each of the six basic intervals" (pp. 27–28).

He begins with the projection of the perfect fifth—one of the two intervals that, superimposed upon itself repeatedly, will eventually produce all elements of the chromatic scale. As an example, the perfect fifth projection on C produces G, then D; this "triad," rearranged to span less than an octave, is C-D-G. Hanson analyzes this sonority, containing two perfect fifths (C to G and G to D) and a major second (C to D), as p^2s (equivalent to set class 3-9 [027]). Similarly, the "perfect-fifth tetrad" is C-G-D-A or C-D-G-A, analyzed as p^3ns^2 (equivalent to sc 4-23 [0257]). (Although Hanson rearranges such projections to fit within an octave, he maintains the starting note, and thus often does not use what is known in set theory as normal order, the most compact possible ordering of the set. The normal order of this tetrachord would be G-A-C-D.) The pentad is $p^4mn^2s^3$ (sc 5-35 [02479], sometimes called the pentatonic scale, collection, or pentachord); the hexad is $p^5m^2n^3s^4d$ (sc 6-32 [024579], often called the diatonic or Guidonian hexachord). Hanson continues this projection until he has derived a complete chromatic scale, or duodecad, which is analyzed as $p^{12}m^{12}n^{12}s^{12}d^{12}t^6$. He points out that in each of these sonorities, in addition to a preponderance of perfect fifths, there is also a respectively smaller preponderance of major seconds, then minor thirds; and that each added tone also adds a new interval until there are seven tones, after which there are no new intervals, but a gradual decrease of the difference in quantity of different intervals. He considers this perhaps the greatest argument against twelve-tone composition, "since such patterns tend to lose their identity, producing a monochromatic effect with its accompanying lack of the essential element of contrast" (p. 33).

As he will continue to do throughout the book, Hanson offers brief examples from the literature, such as the principal C major theme of the "Leonore" Overture no. 3 and the opening "daybreak" theme from the *Daphnis et Chloe* Suite no. 2, both of which he considers to be constructed with the first five tones of the perfect-fifth projection. (In the case of the "Leonore" theme, the notes reduce to C-D-E-G-A, the perfect-fifth projection on C; in the *Daphnis* theme, the notes reduce to E-G-A-B-D, or G-A-B-D-E, the perfect-fifth projection on G.)

A "useful device" of many modern composers is to begin a passage with "only a few tones of a particular projection" and then gradually to add more tones of the same projection. Examples from the opening of Stravinsky's *Petrushka* and Prokofieff's Symphony no. 6 are quoted.

Chapter 5

Since every scale of seven or more tones contains all six interval types, "the student's best opportunity for the study of different types of tone relationship lies in the six-tone combinations" (p. 40); consequently the book concentrates on the various types of hexads. The first five parts of the book are primarily concerned with deriving and analyzing all the types of hexads, as well as all of their constituent subsets.

To begin, Hanson considers the subsets of the "perfect-fifth hexad" (i.e., the hexad created by the first six notes of the perfect-fifth projection), which are defined and differentiated by both their interval analysis—pmd, pmn, etc.—and their interval succession: first, the six types of triads; then, the seven types of tetrads; then, the three pentads. (As he will continue to do in the next chapters, he shows examples of each of the triad, tetrad and pentad types in parallel octaves for playing at the piano, both as arpeggios and as block chords, the latter with some variations in position and doublings. The purpose of these exercises is to help the reader become familiar with the "sound" of each sonority.)

Chapter 6

Hanson borrows the term "modal modulation" to denote the change from one tonal center to another within the same collection of tones. Taking as an example the perfect-fifth hexad on C (C-D-E-G-A-B), Hanson gives a progression beginning on an A minor triad and ending on an E minor triad, using only the six notes of the hexad, to illustrate a modal modulation.

Chapter 7

While modal modulation is "the most subtle and delicate form of modulation," it does not add any tones to the sonority; for this, the composer can resort either to adding more tones to the given tones of a projection, or to "the familiar device of key modulation" (p. 62). With the pentatonic scale, or perfect-fifth pentad (analyzed as $p^4mn^2s^3$), the closest modulation will be to the keys a perfect fifth above or below the tonic, because they will have the most tones in common; the next closest to the keys a major second above or below, then a minor third above or below, and so forth.

Chapter 8

Taking up where he left off in Chapter 4, Hanson considers the minor second, the only other interval besides the perfect fifth whose consistent projection eventually includes all the tones of the chromatic scale. He presents each of the sonorities produced by the addition of another term to the projection; then (in a parallel to Chapter 5) he considers and analyzes the subsets of the minor-second hexad (equivalent to sc 6-1 [012345], commonly known as the chromatic hexachord).

Chapter 9

Hanson continues with the projection of the major second, up to the six-tone scale, or "major-second hexad" (sc 6-35 [02468T], commonly known as the whole-tone collection), and analyzes the subsets of the hexad.

Chapter 10

The major-second scale cannot be extended beyond six tones without repeating itself, but additional tones can be added by arbitrarily selecting a "foreign tone" and projecting major seconds above it. To the major-second scale on C (i.e., C-D-E-F♯-G♯-A♯) Hanson adds G (the perfect fifth) to create a seven-tone scale (C-D-E-F♯-G-G♯-A♯, equivalent to sc 7-33 [012468T]), and adds successive major seconds above G to create eight-tone and larger scales. Then he analyzes the constituent triads. (Hanson later said that his choice of the fifth as the first "foreign" tone in this and subsequent projections was arbitrary, but that the fifth was a good choice because, except for the minor second, it is the only interval that, if continually added, would eventually produce all twelve chromatic tones.)[85]

Chapter 11

Hanson next looks at the projection of the minor third. This collection cannot be extended beyond four tones (C-E♭-G♭-A), so he again adds the perfect fifth and then a minor third above that, then analyzes the constituent subsets of this hexad (C-E♭-G♭-A plus G-B♭, or C-E♭-G♭-G-A-B♭, equivalent to sc 6-27 [013469]). These subsets include two tetrads that Hanson calls isomeric "twins," i.e., they have the same interval analysis but are neither transpositions nor involutions of each other. (In set theory terminology, they are Z-related.)

Hanson follows this with a brief discussion of the difficulties of ascertaining the comparative degree of dissonance between sonorities containing different combinations of intervals, or different numbers of tones. Based on his own (unproven) conclusions, he shows a thirteen-measure musical example in which the harmonies progress from what he considers the most consonant to the most dissonant of the constituent sonorities of the minor-third hexad.

Chapter 12

Hanson considers the involution of the minor-third hexad, which—unlike the hexads of the perfect fifth, minor third and major second—is not isometric (inversionally symmetrical), and analyzes its constituent subsets. These include an isomeric pair, the involutions of the isomeric pair shown in the previous chapter.

Chapter 13

Hanson now extends the projection of the minor third beyond six tones, by adding another two minor thirds above the last tone of the six-tone series, then adding a second "foreign tone" a fifth above the first foreign tone (or a major second above the original tone), and adding three more minor thirds above that—for example, C-E♭-G♭-A plus G-B♭-D♭-F♭ plus D-F-A♭-C♭.

Chapter 14

Hanson now considers the projection of the major third. This can only be extended to three tones, so Hanson again adds the perfect fifth, then two major thirds above that, to form a hexad (C-E-G♯ plus G-B-D♯, or C-D♯-E-G-G♯-B, equivalent to sc 6-20 [014589], commonly known as the hexatonic collection), and then analyzes the constituent subsets.

Chapter 15

Hanson continues the projection of the major third beyond six tones, by adding a second foreign tone a fifth above the first one (or a major second above the original tone) and adding two more major thirds above that, then a third foreign tone a fifth above the second one (or a sixth above the original tone) and two major thirds above that—for example, C-E-G♯ plus G-B-D♯ plus D-F♯-A♯ plus A-C♯-E♯.

Chapter 16

Hanson summarizes the twelve types of "triads" that can be found in the chromatic scale (treating each triad and its involution as a single type), all of which have been previously described in Chapters 5 through 15.

Chapter 17

Hanson now considers the projection of the tritone. He points out that the chromatic scale contains twelve occurrences of each basic interval except the tritone, of which there are only six, and concludes that "the tritone may be said to have twice the *valency* of the other intervals. . . . It is necesssary, therefore, in judging the *relative importance* of the tritone in any scale to multiply the number of tritones by two" (pp. 139–40).

Since the tritone cannot be projected without duplication beyond the original interval, a projection must be formed by superimposing a tritone upon projections that do not already contain tritones. Hanson adds a tritone to each of the first three tones of the perfect-fifth projection to form a hexad. This hexad is identical to the hexad formed by adding a tritone to each of the first three tones of the minor-second projection. (For example, adding tritones to C-G-D results in the ordered scale C-D♭-D-F♯-G-A♭; adding tritones to C-D♭-D results in the same scale.)[86] He then analyzes the component subsets of this "six-tone scale" (equivalent to sc 6-7 [012678], the so-called D-type all-combinatorial hexachord) and discusses its general qualities.

Chapter 18

Hanson continues the perfect-fifth–tritone projection from Chapter 17 by superimposing tritones on the rest of the perfect-fifth hexad.

Chapter 19

Hanson says that, among all of the six-tone sonorities produced by superimposing tritones on the nine triads that do not contain tritones, there is only one sonority that has not already been discussed: the scale produced by superimposing tritones on the three tones of the triad *pmn* (equivalent to sc 3-11 [037], the major or minor triad). He analyzes the constituent subsets of this sonority (C-E-G plus F♯-B♭-C♯, or C-C♯-E-F♯-G-B♭, equivalent to sc 6-30 [013679], sometimes known as the "Petrushka chord").

Chapter 20

Hanson considers the involution of the above sonority and its constituent subsets.

Chapter 21

Hanson summarizes the twenty-nine types of tetrads in the equal-tempered scale, each of which has now been described in previous chapters.

Part II: Construction of Hexads by the Superimposition of Triad Forms

Chapter 22

Having exhausted the projection of single intervals, Hanson turns to the formation of sonorities by "projection" (superimposition) of triads. Beginning with the triad *pmn* (sc 3-11 [037]) he superimposes a major triad on the fifth of a major triad (for example, C-E-G plus G-B-D), then a major triad on the third of the original major triad (for example, C-E-G plus E-G♯-B), then combines the resultant pentads to form the "six-tone major triad projection" or "*pmn* hexad" (C-D-E-G-G♯-B, sc 6-31 [014579]), which "contains the maximum number of major triads" (p. 168).

Chapters 23–26

Hanson proceeds analogously with the triad *pns* (sc 3-7 [025]), superimposing *pns* triads on the upper two tones of the triad and analyzing the components of the resultant six-tone scale, and does likewise with the triad *pmd* (sc 3-4 [015]), the triad *mnd* (sc 3-3 [014]), and the triad *nsd* (sc 3-2 [013]). He then shows that similar projections of the remaining triads produce no new sonorities.

Part III: Six-Tone Scales Formed by the Simultaneous Projection of Two Intervals

Chapter 27

Hanson begins with combinations of the minor third and other intervals, "since these combinations offer the greatest variety of possibilities" (p. 195). First he uses the simultaneous superimposition of three successive perfect fifths and three minor thirds above a fundamental note to form an isometric (inversionally symmetrical) hexad (for example, C-G-D-A plus C-E♭-G♭-A, or C-D-E♭-G♭-G-A, equivalent to sc 6-Z29 [023679]), then analyzes the constituent pentads. Every isometric six-tone scale formed by the projection of two intervals has an isomeric twin; the twin for the above hexad is that produced by superimposing one three-tone minor-third projection on another at the interval of the perfect fifth (for example, C-E♭-G♭ plus G-B♭-D♭, or C-D♭-E♭-G♭-G-B♭, equivalent to sc 6-Z50 [014679]). He analyzes the constituent pentads of the isomeric twin.

Chapter 28

Hanson continues analogously by constructing a new six-tone scale from the combined three-tone minor- and major-third projections, and analyzing its constituent pentads; then he constructs its isomeric twin by superimposing one three-tone minor-third projection on another at the interval of the major third, and analyzing its constituent pentads.

Chapters 29–32

He continues analogously with the six-tone scale formed by the combination of the minor-third and major-second projections, and its isomeric twin; with the combination of the minor-third and minor-second projections, and its isomeric twin; with the combination of the major-third and perfect-fifth projections, and its isomeric twin; and with the combination of the major-third and minor-second projections, and its isomeric twin.

Chapter 33

The analogous combination of the perfect-fifth and minor-second projections does *not* produce an isometric scale, but a scale (for

example, C-G-D-A plus C-C♯-D-D♯, or C-C♯-D-D♯-G-A, sc 6-Z41
[012368]) that has both an involution and an isomeric twin (sc 6-Z12
[012467]) with its own involution. On the other hand, taking the superimposition of two perfect-fifth projections at the interval of the
minor second (for example, C-G-D plus D♭-A♭-E♭, or C-D♭-D-E♭-G-A♭,
sc 6-Z38 [012378])—which in the earlier cases produced an isomeric
twin of the first hexad (see the summary of Chapter 27 above)—*does*
produce an isomeric scale, with an isomeric twin that can be produced by "reversing the projection," i.e., superimposing two minor-
second projections at the interval of the perfect fifth (i.e., C-C♯-D plus
G-G♯-A, sc 6-Z6 [012567]).

Part IV: Projection by Involution and at Foreign Intervals

Chapter 34

Here Hanson formally discusses the concept (already introduced without explanation in previous chapters) of the projection of
one or more intervals simultaneously above and below a starting
tone (or "projection by involution"). Simultaneously projecting any
two intervals above and below a tone always produces an isometric
pentad; the only way to produce an isometric hexad is to add a tritone. All of the hexads thus produced have been previously discussed
(in Chapters 18–21).

Chapter 35

Hanson examines the six-tone subsets of the "seven-tone major-
second scale" (for example, C-D-E-F♯-G-G♯-A♯, derived in Chapter
10), and offers various analyses of the "impure major-second
scales" (i.e., those other than the whole-tone scale).

Chapter 36

Some of the six-tone scales already discussed can be analyzed
in several ways, for instance as the projection of a triad, not at an
interval included in the triad, but at a "foreign" interval. An example would be the projection of a triad *pmn* (for example, C-E-G) at the
interval *s* (a major second), i.e., C-E-G plus D-F♯-A, or C-D-E-F♯-G-
A (equivalent to sc 6-22 [012468]). In this way Hanson considers the
six-tone scales that have not already been described.

Chapter 37

Hanson summarizes the thirty-eight pentad types, all of which have now been described, with their involutions.

Part V: The Theory of Complementary Sonorities

Chapter 38

The six tones not included within any hexad constitute a complementary hexad. When the original hexad is isometric, the complement is either a transposition of the original, or its isomeric twin. When the original hexad is not isometric, the complement is either its involution, or a slightly more complex type covered in the next chapter.

Chapter 39

In the last case referred to in the previous paragraph, the original hexad and its isomeric complement each have their own involution, and all four hexads have the same interval analysis. Hanson calls these "quartets of hexads"; he presents each of these eight quartets and their analyses. All but one of these can be derived from the projection of triads at foreign intervals (as presented in Chapter 36).

Part VI: Complementary Scales

Chapter 40

Hanson extends the concept of complementarity introduced in Part V to all sonorities. Every sonority has a complementary sonority consisting of the remaining tones of the twelve-tone scale, and the complementary sonority always has the same "type" of interval analysis as the original, i.e., the same interval(s) will be preponderant. Hanson gives the example of the complement of the major triad, a nine-tone scale which has a preponderance of perfect fifths, major thirds, and minor thirds—the same three intervals that constitute the major triad. Analyzing this scale in terms of the projection of a triad, he demonstrates that the nine-tone "projection" of a triad is the involution of the triad's complementary scale, and shows a quick way to ascertain the "projection" of any sonority (the "projection" being the sonority with the complementary number of tones, modulo 12)—in other words, a way to ascertain, for any sonority of cardinality n, its projection with cardinality $12-n$: to take the involution of the sonority's complement, beginning at the original starting tone. Hanson then considers the question of whether composers use such analytical considerations while writing, and answers "consciously—no, subconsciously—yes" (p. 272).

Chapter 41

Hanson begins his presentation of the projection-by-complement with the basic intervals. He presents a table with all the sonorities of the perfect-fifth projection and their complements, from the basic perfect-fifth doad with its complementary decad, through the decad (the involution of the doad's complementary decad) and its complementary doad, to the undecad (the eleven-tone projection, of which there is only one type) and the duodecad (the twelve-tone projection, of which there is also only one type). Then he proceeds analogously with the minor-second projection, the major-second projection, the minor-third projection, the major-third projection, and the tritone projection.

Chapter 42

Hanson now turns to the projection-by-complement of the triad projections, beginning with the sonorities of the projection of the major triad *pmn* (sc 3-11 [037]), followed by those of the triads *pns* (sc 3-7 [025]), *pmd* (sc 3-4 [015]), *mnd* (sc 3-3 [014]), and *nsd* (sc 3-2 [013]). (Appendix H shows a reproduction of the *pns* projection.)

Chapter 43

Hanson proceeds analogously with the *pmn*-tritone projection, as discussed in Chapter 19 (for example, C-E-G plus F♯-A♯-C♯, or C-C♯-E-F♯-G-A♯, sc 6-30 [013679], the "Petrushka chord"), which "offers possibilities of great tonal beauty to composers who are intrigued with the sound of the tritone" (p. 296).

Chapter 44

Hanson proceeds analogously with the projection of tetrads composed of two similar intervals at a "foreign" interval (i.e., of a single interval x projected at another interval y)—for example, taking the tetrad C-E-G-B, composed of the perfect-fifth projections C-G and

E-B at the interval of the major third. Projecting this tetrad at the interval of the major third, i.e., C-E-G-B plus E-G♯-B-D♯, produces the hexad C-D♯-E-G-G♯-B (sc 6-20 [014589], the hexatonic collection). The choice of x or y for the interval at which to project is dictated by avoiding the one that would produce a sonority belonging to an isomeric pair or "quartet," all of which have already been described in Chapters 38 and 39.

Chapter 45

Hanson proceeds analogously with the simultaneous projection of two different intervals from a common starting tone: first the fifth and the major second (for example, C-G plus C-D, producing C-D-G), then the minor second and major second, then the fifth and the minor second, the fifth and the minor second in opposite directions, the major second and the major third, the fifth and the major third, the minor second and major third, the fifth and minor third, the fifth and minor third in opposite directions, the minor second and minor third, the minor second and minor third in opposite directions, the major second and minor third, the major second and minor third in opposite directions, the major and minor third, and the major and minor third in opposite directions. Finally he shows the simultaneous projection of three intervals: the fifth, the major second, and the minor second.

Chapter 46

Hanson reintroduces the idea from Chapter 34 that an isometric series, such as the projection of the perfect fifth, can be explained as the simultaneous projection of fifths "above" and "below" a given axis on the circle of fifths (for example, projecting from C "above" to G and "below" to F, relative to the axis C–F♯), instead of as the superposition of a single interval. While such considerations for a single interval offer only a different way of looking at the same results, "projection by involution" of two different intervals produces new sonorities. Hanson gives the example of projecting perfect fifths above and below a starting tone, followed by the projection of major thirds, in contrast to the projection of major thirds followed by perfect fifths, which produces the same pentads, hexads and heptads, but has different triads, tetrads, octads and nonads. (To clarify: In the first case Hanson begins with fifths above and below a starting tone, then adds a major third either above the tone, which produces a tetrad—for example, C-G plus C-F plus C-E, producing C-E-F-G—or below the tone, which produces a different tetrad that is the involution of the first tetrad—for example, C-G plus C-F plus C-A♭, producing C-F-G-A♭. In set-theory terms, the first tetrachord is {0,4,5,7}, a member of sc 4-14 [0237], and the second is {0,5,7,8}, also a member of sc 4-14, and an inverted transposition of the first tetrachord. Then Hanson takes the thirds both above *and* below, which produces a pentad, and so forth. On the other hand, to begin with major thirds above and below the tone, and then add a fifth either above or below, creates two other tetrads. For example, C-E plus C-A♭ plus C-G produces C-E-G-A♭, while C-E plus C-A♭ plus C-F produces C-E-F-A♭; these tetrads are also inverted transpositions of each other, members of sc 4-19 [0148]. However, adding fifths both above *and* below creates the same pentad as in the first case, and so forth.) This is followed by the similar projections of perfect fifths and minor thirds; perfect fifths and minor seconds; major and minor thirds; major thirds and minor seconds; and minor thirds and minor seconds. The other such combinations duplicate projections already presented, with a single exception discussed in the next chapter.

Chapter 47

The projection by involution of minor thirds and major seconds (for example, minor thirds above and below C, or A-C-E♭, and major seconds above and below C, or B♭-C-D) forms an anomaly (the pentad C-D-E♭-A-B♭, equivalent to sc 5-Z12 [01356]) that Hanson calls the "maverick" sonority. This projection is unique, in that the involution of the complement of its pentad, a "heptad" or seven-tone scale, does not contain the pentad as a subset. (In every other case, the complementary heptad does contain the original pentad, albeit sometimes transposed and inverted, plus two additional tones.) The heptad that *does* contain the pentad is the involution of the complement of the pentad's isomeric twin, while the twin pentad is contained in the involution of both its own *and* its twin's complements. (This twin pentad is equivalent to sc 5-Z36 [01247].)

Chapter 48

Continuing projection by involution, with the aid of a slightly modified diagram of the circle of fifths, Hanson shows that of the ten possible pentads involving projection of two (different) intervals above and below a central note, both of the projected intervals are contained in the complementary heptads of four, but not in the other six. He shows connections between the former and the latter to explain how the eight hexad "quartets" from Chapter 39 can be derived.

In the latter half of the chapter he shows how the twenty-six isomeric-twin hexads can be derived from various combinations of interval projections.

Chapter 49

Hanson explains the use of the diagram at the back of the book, a large foldout insert entitled "The Projection and Interrelation of Sonorities in Equal Temperament," which he considers the most complete presentation of the tonal relationships described in the book, although he emphasizes that he is concerned "not with symbolism but with *sound*." (The diagram appears in this book, considerably reduced, as Appendix A. On the foldout insert in *Harmonic Materials*, the diagram measures $17\frac{1}{2}$ by 21 inches.) This diagram, a large symmetrical structure, beginning with the "doads" at the lower right and ending with the "decads" at the upper right, has a unique row for each sonority, which is listed by its "projection" derivation, followed by its interval analysis and its interval succession. Each sonority is placed symmetrically opposite its complement, except for the hexads, where complements are placed one above the other. The diagram shows, by the intersection of rows and columns, which intervals are included in each triad, which triads are included in each tetrad, and so forth.

"For the sake of space the interval analysis . . . is given as six numbers, without the interval letters *p, m, n, s, d,* and *t*" (p. 349). For example, $p^6m^3n^4s^5d^2t$, the interval analysis of the sonority P^6, is shown on the diagram as 634,521; this can be seen, when the diagram is rotated 90° clockwise, in the lowest row of the second-highest horizontal block, with the Roman numeral VII to its left, representing the heptads. (As Janet Schmalfeldt among others has pointed out, this means that the interval analyses appearing in Hanson's diagram are virtually identical to Allen Forte's interval vectors, which first appeared four years later.[87] For instance, the P^6 sonority, with the interval analysis 634,521 in Hanson's diagram, is equivalent to sc 7-35 [013568T], with the interval vector 254361, in Forte's set list. The only differences are in the ordering—Forte reverses the order of Hanson's first five intervals—and in Hanson's use of a comma between the first three interval values and the last three.)

According to Hanson, the diagram reveals a great amount of information about tonal relationships, and he gives the example of how to derive the interval analysis of the complement of any sonority by adding a constant (which depends on the number of elements in the original sonority) to each element of the interval analysis of the original sonority. For instance, the interval analysis of a tetrad's complementary octad can be found by adding four to each element of the tetrad's interval analysis, except that only half of that, or two, is added to the tritone's interval count, as Hanson has explained in Chapter 17. As an example, the interval analysis of the tetrad C-D-G-A is 301,200; adding 4 to each interval except the tritone, and adding 2 to the tritone, produces 745,642, the analysis of the complementary octad. In Appendix A, this can be seen (without the clockwise rotation) in the lowest row of the highest section that runs horizontally across both pages (i.e., the twenty-ninth row below the Roman numerals VIII and IV near the top of the two pages), with the tetrad (P^3) to the right of center, and the octad to the left.[88]

Chapter 50

Hanson translates the essence of the foldout diagram into musical notation—each sonority shown linearly on a separate musical staff—with the understanding that each staff stands for many others not notated. For example, a nine-tone scale can have nine different versions, depending on rotation, i.e., on which note of the scale is taken as the starting note; if it has an involution, the involution will also have nine versions; and each version can be transposed to every note of the chromatic scale, so that one scale type shown in the text can represent as many as 216 different scales.

Hanson begins with the twelve-tone and eleven-tone scales, each of which has only one type, followed by the six ten-tone scales (all isometric) and their complementary intervals, in the order presented in the chart. Then follow the twelve nine-tone scales with their involutions, and their complementary triads with involutions; the twenty-nine octads and tetrads; the thirty-eight heptads and pentads; and the fifty hexads (with isomeric twins and quartets being presented as variants on the same line). A sample page of Chapter 50 is reproduced in this book as Appendix B.

In conclusion Hanson mentions how, in the first four measures of the song "En Svane" by Grieg, the sound is changed "from its gentle pastoral quality to one of vague foreboding" by the changing of a single note. "If this text is of any help in assisting the young composer to find the *right* note, the labor of writing it will not have been in vain."

Appendix: Symmetrical Twelve-Tone Forms

Hanson adds, as possibly useful to composers wishing to write dodecaphonic music, a list of nineteen hexads which form symmetrical scales with their complementary involutions. (For several he gives more than one involution, depending on the choice of "converting tone" or starting tone for the involution.) He points out that for each such scale, the first n tones (where $7 \leq n \leq 12$) always form the complementary projection of the first $12-n$ tones, and that this is true regardless of the order of tones in the original hexad.

Chapter 4

The Theory Considered as a System

HISTORICAL SKETCH

Readers familiar with contemporary music theory will already have been struck by the extraordinary similarity between many aspects of the theory presented in *Harmonic Materials* and the body of scholarly literature known as musical set theory. As developed and codified by such writers as Milton Babbitt, David Lewin, Donald Martino, and Allen Forte, this theory has become well known and influential in academic circles during the last forty years.[89] Before making a comparison of the two theories, however, it will be useful to reconstruct their chronological context. Although the entire history of the development of theories attempting to classify all possible combinations of tones is beyond the scope of this book, a brief look at the antecedents and consequents of Hanson's theory will help to illuminate its historical significance.[90]

As is not uncommon in the history of ideas, elements of such theories had been in the air, so to speak, for some time before Hanson wrote *Harmonic Materials*. It would not be too fanciful to say that the various attempts made during the first sixty years of the twentieth century to catalog all the possible combinations of tones in the chromatic scale—a task that had been theoretically possible to accomplish at least as early as 1700—were part of a trend among scholars of reaching toward vast general syntheses or all-embracing unified theories, as Albert Einstein and others attempted to do in physics, and Arnold Schoenberg and Josef Hauer in their twelve-tone systems. Certainly it is true that elements of a comprehensive theory of tonal relations and intervals began to appear even before the turn of the century. At some time around the year 1894, the pseudonymous H. J. Vincent—in his provocatively-titled pamphlet *Ist unsere Harmonielehre wirklich eine Theorie?*—had made early use of integer notation, with zero representing the tonic note in any arbitrarily selected key, and had used a concept of "interval" that approximated a pitch-class interval (although a directed one).[91] German theorists also showed interest in the concept of symmetrical or "mirror" inversion of harmonies, and within the first few years of the twentieth century, books by Hermann Schröder (*Die symmetrische Umkehrung in der Musik*, 1902), Georg Capellen (*Ein neuer exotischer Musikstil*, 1906) and Bernhard Ziehn (*Canonical Studies*, 1912) explored this subject. Schröder also discussed the concepts of transpositional and inversional equivalence.

Soon after this came a spurt of activity, now explicitly directed toward a reckoning and tallying of all the potential groupings of the chromatic collection, in both Europe and America. In 1917, the American composer Ernst Bacon correctly enumerated all transpositionally equivalent "harmonies" (T_n types of sets) of cardinalities two through twelve, implicitly incorporating the concept of pitch class. Although he differentiated between scalar (ordered) and harmonic (unordered) groupings, did not utilize inversional equivalence, and made no reckoning of interval content, this was clearly an important step toward a complete theory of potential chromatic collections.[92] Josef Hauer, in a 1922 article that followed up on his earlier work on twelve-tone theory and first proposed his concept of hexachordal "tropes," arrived at an equivalent count for the hexachords, although there were similar limitations in his methods.[93] In 1925 Fritz Heinrich Klein, a composition student of Alban Berg, gave a correct count of the total number of all distinct "fundamental chords" (*Urklänge*, equivalent to pitch-class sets, but not to set classes), and provided complete lists of dyads and trichords; and in 1927 Alois Hába attempted, among other things, to catalog all possible combinations of chromatic tones, although a scattershot and inconsistent method meant that his list contained both redundancies and omissions.[94]

In 1946, Milton Babbitt's doctoral dissertation utilized several characteristics of the group concept from mathematics as a model for what he called a "set." Here and subsequently Babbitt used the term "set" to refer to an ordered twelve-tone row, albeit one in which the first and second halves could be considered unordered hexachords, like Hauer's tropes.[95] He summarized this concept in an article, published in 1955, that discussed the use of hexachordal and tetrachordal combinatoriality as a basis for serial and "total serial" composition. Like several later articles by Babbitt on sets, this article was exclusively concerned with twelve-tone music.[96] Other writers, however, inspired by the basic concept of the musical set and the focus on hexachords and smaller subsets of the twelve-tone collection, later took these ideas in new directions that led to the development of musical set theory. An almost equally seminal article by David Lewin, dealing with the "intervallic relations between collections of notes"—in which the term "note," like Hanson's term "tone," was essentially equivalent to what came to be called pitch class—appeared in 1959.[97] This article also had no bearing on set theory *per se*, although five months later Lewin was to publish a second article in which he developed further the concepts presented in this article, and produced results that became important aspects of set theory.

But in the meantime, early in 1960, Howard Hanson's *Harmonic Materials of Modern Music* had been published. Exactly when Hanson first began to work on the theory that he expounded in *Harmonic Materials* is not and may never be clear. His own memory on the subject was not completely reliable, perhaps because, as he put it in 1978, "I think I've been fooling around with it all of my life, really."[98] While there is no concrete evidence that this was literally true, it is quite plausible that Hanson was referring to a lifelong interest in intervals and harmonic relationships, beginning perhaps as early as his Northwestern University thesis "Upon Temperament and Scale-Construction," written when he was nineteen.[99] At another point in the same series of interviews he mentioned "working . . . for forty years on that theory"; counting backward from the publication of *Harmonic Materials,* this would seem to confirm an origin around 1920. On the other hand, at yet another point in the interviews he said, "I think I must have started it somewhere around 1940. . . . It must have been at least 1940, or maybe even before, when I began."[100] This seems to contradict the earlier statements, unless we posit a rather unlikely distinction in Hanson's mind between "fooling around with" the theory (which would therefore be equivalent to "working on" the theory) and "starting" it with the intention of codifying and publishing it.

A more plausible explanation for the discrepancy can be found if we make the distinction between "fooling around" on the one hand, and "working on" and "starting" on the other: Hanson may have meant that he had worked on the theory not only in the years prior to publication, but also in the years afterward. Not only did he make use of the theory in his later compositions (as will be discussed in the sixth and seventh chapters of this book), but, as we will see shortly, for the rest of his life he continued to work on revisions to *Harmonic Materials*, and to ponder and experiment with scales, sonorities and projections. If this interpretation is correct, it would again place the origin of the theory around 1940. On the other hand, earlier statements on the subject seem to indicate an origin in the early 1930s. In his 1948 lectures at Harvard, he mentioned that he had already been working on the theory "for the past fifteen years"; in 1960, when *Harmonic Materials* was published, an article in a Rochester newspaper referred to it as a project on which Hanson had worked "for some 30 years"; the first sentence in the book's Preface says that it was the result of "over a quarter-century of study"; and in his unfinished autobiography, written in the late 1960s, he wrote that he had begun "as long as forty years ago an intensive study of the resources of the twelve-tone chromatic scale."[101] All of the above discrepancies can be explained if we interpret these various statements to mean that he had been thinking about interval relationships for most of his life, that he began to develop the theory around 1930, and that he started working seriously on codifying it and putting it into a coherent written form around 1940. In any case, by the mid-1940s Hanson had developed the theory far enough that he began to use concepts and techniques from it in his teaching, and a number of his students remembered him discussing the theory in seminars and using it in advanced composition classes by the late 1940s.[102]

The publication of the theory took Hanson much longer than he had expected. Its first mention in print seems to have been in a *Musical America* article about Hanson's induction into the American Philosophical Society. At the induction ceremony in November 1951, Hanson read a paper entitled "The Projection and Inter-Relation of Sonorities in Equal Temperament." It is clear that this paper was a brief summary of what would become *Harmonic Materials*, not only from its title but from its description in the article as "a new theory for the analyzing of musical sonorities. . . . The result of more than ten years of study, the analysis groups all possible series of tones in the twelve-tone divisions of the octave, assigning them to categories according to the preponderance of certain elements and of consonance and dissonance." Hanson illustrated his talk with a five-by-six-foot chart showing interval relationships.[103] This chart was presumably an earlier and larger version of the foldout master diagram at the back of *Harmonic Materials*, which bears the same title as the 1951 paper. At that point Hanson expected the book to be published in 1952, but it was not until 1954 or 1955 that he completed the book in typescript, presumably due to revisions he had made in the interim. (The revisions will be discussed later in this chapter.) By this time the theory had reached what seems essentially to have been its final form.[104] In 1956 he expected it to be published by early 1957, although the actual publication took another three years—a not uncommon occurrence in publishing, especially with a book containing many illustrations and a foldout insert.

Within weeks of the publication of *Harmonic Materials*, David Lewin's second article on intervallic relations appeared, in the April 1960 issue of the *Journal of Music Theory*.[105] In this article, using a self-reflexive form of the "interval function" he had introduced the previous year, Lewin produced a version of what later became known as the "interval vector" of set theory, although using intervals rather than interval classes. Lewin also proved the theorem that all hexachords and their complements have the same interval content, and identified certain pairs of collections that have identical interval content but are neither transpositions nor inversions of each other, which later became known in Forte's terminology as Z-related set classes. (These pairs had, of course, already been identified and described, as the "isomeric twins" and "quartets," by Hanson.)

In 1964 Allen Forte's first major article on set-class theory appeared, in which he set forth many of the concepts, terms, and procedures that have defined the field ever since.[106] A number of aspects of his initial presentation provoked debate among interested theorists, and nine years later, after some significant revisions, Forte published an expanded version of his theory in a book that is still considered a classic work in its field.[107]

The preceding historical sketch aptly illustrates the notion that theoretical ideas often seem to be in the air at a certain historical moment. Two well-known examples are the independent development of calculus by Isaac Newton and Gottfried Leibniz within a few years of 1670, and the independent development of twelve-tone compositional methods by Schoenberg and Hauer within a few years of 1920. As in these cases, similar ideas and concepts of tonal relations seem to have been developed independently by a number of musical thinkers in Europe and America in the period between 1940 and 1960. Still, when one considers how extremely dissimilar, if not contrary, were the premises and concerns from which Hanson and set theorists such as Babbitt, Lewin or Forte started, it is remarkable that they produced work with so much in common, within a few years of each other.

From another perspective, of course, the similarities should hardly be surprising: any complete, systematic, and accurate classification of the intervallic constitution of the chromatic collection and its subsets should lead to similar results, no matter what concepts or terms are used. Nevertheless, the fact remains that many of the concepts and rules of set-class theory were arrived at first and published first, though with different and mostly nonmathematical terminology, by Hanson.[108] The first to treat pitch-class sets (or "sonorities") related by transposition or inversion as equivalent, and the first to calculate correctly the interval vector (or "interval analysis") for each such set class, he was also the first to correctly classify and list all of them, and to identify or describe many of their important properties and relations.[109]

EVALUATION AND COMPARISON

Any contemporary evaluation of Hanson's theory must entail some comparison with set theory, although an exhaustive, point-by-point comparison is unnecessary. But it will be useful first to evaluate Hanson's theory on its own terms, with only occasional reference to set theory, and then to summarize the most important differences between them. (Each specific example cited below can be taken as representative of a number of similar instances.)

Disregarding small points that are clearly either auctorial slips or typographical errors, let us first examine some of the assumptions, explicit and implicit, underlying Hanson's theory. These include octave, inversional and enharmonic equivalence; the ignoring of such distinctions as bass note, register, doubling, or voice-leading; the equivalence of sonorities that are transpositions and/or inversions of each other; and the treatment of pitches as tones (pitch classes). Such assumptions are unexceptional for an abstract system of tonal relationships—the concept of set class includes all of them, for instance—but there are composers and theorists who continue to question their indiscriminate application to all compositional contexts.[110] Such questions are even more pertinent for a theory that purports to deal as much with tonal as with atonal music, and that claims its ultimate standard to be what the ear actually hears, rather than nonacoustical abstractions. The above assumptions may be necessary for a theory encompassing all possible combinations of chromatic tones, but Hanson does not make the limitations of such a theory clear. In fact, Hanson's assertion that his theory can "analyze factually any passage or phrase written in the twelve-tone equally tempered scale" can be taken to imply that, within the bounds of the chromatic collection, the theory has no limitations. This is unfortunate because the analysis of music, such as Hanson's own, that relies to any extent on functional harmony—for instance, on dominant-tonic progressions—cannot ignore such considerations as bass note, register, or inversion. The greater the use of functional relationships, the less convincing is an analysis based on the above assumptions.[111]

A simple illustration of this can be found even in Hanson's *For the First Time* (1963), a piece that was written, in part, to illustrate aspects of his theory, and containing comparatively few of the triadic harmonies that pervade many of his works. Example 4.1 shows the last two measures of the piece in the piano solo version.

Example 4.1   Hanson, *For the First Time,* "Dreams," mm. 41–42

This ending differs from a conventional V–I cadence in the absence of a B from the last beat of the penultimate measure, and the presence of a suspended D (which most listeners would probably hear as a major ninth) in the final measure, but it clearly fulfills a similar function. If doubling or the choice of bass notes were irrelevant to the ear, this ending would have no greater feeling of finality than if there were only a single C in a treble octave in the final measure and an E or D in the bass. Similarly, if the intervals of the fifth and the fourth were equivalent in sound, the ending would be just as effective with one C in the treble and a G (or several Gs) in the bass.[112] Clearly neither is the case. It is true that Hanson provides a different viewpoint in a note where he speculates on "the reason why two sonorities containing identical tones should sound so differently," and as an example he compares a chord that is essentially a G major triad over a C major triad with a chord that is essentially a C major triad over a G major triad. Although Hanson's language in this note is extremely vague, in essence he speculates that the former sonority is more pleasing, or consonant, because the tones are heard in relative positions that more closely approximate those of the natural harmonic series.[113] However, there is no systematic discussion of these issues. Years later, Hanson said that the one aspect of *Harmonic Materials* that he would change was that "I was too casual in saying that inversions and the original position are the same thing. . . . They really are not. . . . I think I took that whole thing too lightly, and . . . I find that I would like to tie down a lot of things more."[114] He did not specify what changes such a revision would involve, and although he implied that he was in the process of working on it at the time, the revision was never published.[115]

As suggested in the previous paragraph, the assumption of inversional equivalence is also problematic for a theory whose author asserts that "A sonority sounds as it does primarily because of the relative degree of consonance and dissonance of its elements."[116] The perfect fifth has traditionally been considered the most consonant of intervals after the octave, while the perfect fourth has traditionally been considered dissonant or at least ambiguous. To call them equivalent in tonally-oriented music is to adulterate the concept of consonance. Unfortunately, despite his assertion of its importance, Hanson never gives a clear and consistent definition of consonance. Considering the primacy that Hanson attaches to consonance and dissonance, his failure to make their comparative determination a part of his theory is one of the most puzzling omissions of *Harmonic Materials*. While he does discuss the question, this discussion is not only extremely brief but, as he himself acknowledges, inconclusive.[117] Furthermore, he never explains the ordering of his interval analyses (interval vectors), beyond asserting that the first three positions (p, m, and n) are consonant and the last three (s, d, and t) are dissonant. This would imply that the intervals are listed in order of increasing dissonance, but Hanson himself calls the tritone a "mild dissonance" and the minor second "highly dissonant," and this ordering also ignores the ambiguous nature of the fourth.[118] Even the assumption of enharmonic equivalence is not as self-evidently valid for tonal music as it is for atonal music. In tonal music, with functional harmony and modulation between tonal centers, enharmonics often do not sound equivalent to composers, performers or listeners.[119]

We might also question certain features of Hanson's theory that, though less fundamental, are still important, such as the logic, coherence, and clarity of its presentation. In both the small and the large scale, aspects of this presentation in *Harmonic Materials* are confusing. For instance, in Chapter 38 Hanson begins his discussion of complementarity by dividing the hexads (hexachords) into four categories, based on their type of complementarity. The hexads of the first group are isometric (inversionally symmetrical), and their complements are simple transpositions; each hexad has the same interval analysis (interval vector) as its complement. Those of the second group are not isometric, and their complements are involutions (inversions); each hexad has the same interval analysis as its complement. Those of the third group are not isometric, and their complements are neither transpositions nor inversions, but each hexad has the same interval analysis as its complement; those of the fourth group (the "isomeric twins") are isometric, but their complements are neither transpositions nor inversions, although each hexad has the same interval analysis as its complement. Although Hanson does not give a count of each group, the first group includes six hexads (equivalent to set classes 6-1, 6-7, 6-8, 6-20, 6-32, and 6-35), the second group includes thirteen (6-2, 6-5, 6-9, 6-15, 6-16, 6-18, 6-21, 6-22, 6-27, 6-30, 6-31, 6-33, and 6-34), the third group includes eighteen (6-Z3, 6-Z10, 6-Z11, 6-Z12, 6-Z17, 6-Z19, 6-Z23, 6-Z24, 6-Z25, 6-Z36, 6-Z39, 6-Z40, 6-Z41, 6-Z43, 6-Z44, 6-Z45, 6-Z46, and 6-Z47), and the fourth group includes twelve (6-Z4, 6-Z6, 6-Z13, 6-Z26, 6-Z28, 6-Z29, 6-Z37, 6-Z38, 6-Z42, 6-Z48, 6-Z49, and 6-Z50).[120] However, Hanson neither elaborates on nor explains the difference between these last two cases until the beginning of his next chapter; and in fact Chapter 39 is not an exploration of the fourth and last case, the "isomeric twins" (already dealt with in Chapters 27 through 33), but of the *third* case, the isomeric "hexad quartets." (In the summary of Hanson's Chapter 38 in the third chapter of this book, I listed the "quartets" last because this makes Hanson's classification clearer, but my listing does not reflect the order of presentation in *Harmonic Materials* itself.) It is indeed puzzling that Hanson does not list the "quartets" as his last case, either from considerations of parallelism—thus making his order isometric/equivalent, nonisometric/equivalent, isometric/nonequivalent, nonisometric/nonequivalent—or because logically one would expect him to save the topic on which he is about to expound (in the next chapter) for last. More fundamentally, it might be asked why Hanson makes a point of differentiating between the "twins" and the "quartets," when throughout the book he considers involutions (inversions) as equivalent to their original forms. The set-class concept makes no such distinctions; all of these hexachords are considered Z-related pairs. Given the significance in Hanson's theory of the distinction between isometric and nonisometric sonorities, it is possible that this may not always be a trivial distinction. Nevertheless, he does not explain why he makes more of it here than elsewhere in the book.

There is an additional problem with Hanson's four categories. He clearly implies that these four groups include all the hexads. He also implies, although he does not actually state, that only isometric hexads have complements that are simple transpositions of the originals (the first of the four categories of Chapter 38). However, he has forgotten the hexad *pmd/n*, which is equivalent to sc 6-14 [013458].

This fiftieth, unique hexad, which he illustrates as C-D-E♭-G-B♭-B on page 237 of *Harmonic Materials*, is not isometric—its interval succession is 2-1-4-3-1-1—but its complement (F♯-G♯-A-C♯-E-F) is a transposition at the tritone, and thus it does not fall into any of Hanson's four categories.[121]

Most puzzling of all, however, is that Hanson never states as a general rule that *all* hexachords have the same interval analysis (interval vector) as their complements, although in effect he has shown that this is the case. This failure to draw a general conclusion from specific cases, which occurs in a number of places in *Harmonic Materials,* will be discussed further below.

Another example of confusion can be found in Chapter 47, in which Hanson discusses the pentad C-D-E♭-A-B♭ (equivalent to sc 5-Z12 [01356]) which he nicknames the "maverick sonority" because it is the only sonority (of cardinality less than that of its complement) that is not a "part" (subset) of its complement. While this is true, however, what Hanson actually says is that "it is the only sonority in all of the tonal material of the twelve-tone scale" that is not a subset of its complement. Not only does this assertion omit the necessary qualification that a sonority must be of a cardinality less than or equal to its complement in order to be a subset, but it also ignores an entire class of sonorities that are not subsets of their complements, namely all hexads (hexachords) which are not functionally equivalent to their complements (the third and fourth cases in Hanson's Chapter 38, discussed above—i.e., all of the Z-related hexachords). It could, of course, be argued that for a hexad to be a subset of a hexad is a trivial case, but Hanson does not even deal with the issue. Nor is it possible to tell whether, in making the statement above, he chose to ignore all the hexads, or forgot that many of them have the same property as his "maverick sonority."[122]

Yet another problematic aspect of Hanson's theory is his idiosyncratic terminology. The fact that it has never been used by more than a small number of scholars—mostly graduates of the Eastman School and their students—is due as much to its being virtually unknown as to any flaws in his system *per se.* Even so, his theory is hampered by a lack of clarity and consistency in the definitions of some of his most important terms. He uses the terms "scale" and "sonority" interchangeably, to refer sometimes to T_n-equivalent sets and sometimes to set classes, and often uses the term "scale" when it is inaccurate and misleading—to choose two examples at random, the six-tone collections that serve as his Example 31-1, p. 211 (C-D-E-G-G♯-A), and Example 32-1, p. 215 (C-C♯-D-D♯-E-G♯), which at best might be called "gapped scales." Another example is his definition of the term "involution":

> Every sonority in music has a counterpart obtained by tak-
> ing the *inverse ratio* of the original sonority. The projection
> *down* from the lowest tone of a given chord, using the same
> intervals in the order of their occurrence in the given chord,
> we may call the *involution* of the given chord.[123]

The meaning of this can be deduced with some effort, but the lack of
rigor and clarity in this definition is typical of many of Hanson's
definitions. A similar example is Hanson's use of the term "isometric," which is first mentioned as one of the three types of involution, in which "the involuted sonority has the same kind of sound as
the original sonority."[124] This in itself is extremely vague, although Hanson furnishes an example that makes clear that an
"isometric" involution is a transposition of the original at an interval other than one or more octaves. However, on the next page
Hanson defines an isometric sonority as one that has "the same order of intervals whether considered 'up' or 'down,' clockwise or
counterclockwise." This definition of isometry as, in effect, inversional symmetry is unrelated to Hanson's use of the term on the
previous page, and his use of both meanings throughout the book
adds an element of confusion.

The most crucial concerns about
Hanson's terminology and about the order and mode of presentation
in *Harmonic Materials* revolve around the concept of "projection," a
central and fundamental element of the theory. Up to this point most
of the flaws alluded to, though not insignificant, have been relatively minor, in the sense that they could have been rectified or modified without fundamental alteration to the theory, if the theory had
received the degree of attention and interest that set theory received
as it evolved. In such a case, other writers might have amended
Hanson's work in a way that added to the corpus of the theory, much
as other writers have extended and modified the early work of
Babbitt and Forte in set theory. Even the inherent contradiction between the underlying assumptions of Hanson's theory (such as inversional and enharmonic equivalence) and his claims for it as a
method of analysis of both atonal and tonal music might have been
resolved.

The concept of projection is different, however. It is central to
Hanson's theory, and it determines the entire structure of *Harmonic Materials,* on both the large and the small scale. On the large
scale, the sections and chapters of the book are arranged so that the
various sonorities are presented in order of increasing complexity
of the projections that produce them—first the projections of single
intervals, then the projections of triads, and so forth; and on the

small scale, the form in which each sonority is presented (i.e., the ordering, the choice of which pitch class is chosen as the first and lowest note of a linear array) is determined by the projection from which it is derived, rather than by consistent standards of intervallic size as in the "normal order" and "prime form" of set theory.

The first problem with the concept of projection, as with other terms of Hanson's, is the inconsistency and vagueness of its meaning. It is first defined in the Preface as "the construction of scales or chords by any logical and consistent process of addition and repetition," which could—and, as the book proceeds, does—denote any of a number of possible operations.[125] In Chapter 4 projection is defined as "the building of sonorities or scales by superimposing a series of *similar* intervals one above the other" (although it quickly becomes evident that by "similar" Hanson actually means "identical").[126] As the book goes on, however, he extends the concept further and further. In Chapter 5 he introduces the "projection" of two *different* intervals above a tone (for example, C-D-E-G as the combination of the projection of two perfect fifths C-G-D, plus the projection of two major seconds C-D-E) and the "projection" of the same interval above two *different* tones (for example, C-E-G-A as the combination of either two perfect fifths—A-E plus C-G—at the interval of a minor third, or of two minor thirds—A-C plus E-G—at the interval of a perfect fifth). In Chapter 22, he discusses the "projection" of two intervals *downward* rather than upward, and in Chapter 23, he adds the "projection" of one interval *above* a tone, and a different interval *below* it—despite the fact that a combination of a downward with an upward projection is as different from two upward projections as an undertone is from an overtone. As an example, projecting a major third and perfect fifth above a tone produces the *pmn* triad or sc 3-11 [037], while projecting a major third above, and a fifth below, produces *pmd* or sc 3-4 [015].

In Chapter 35 Hanson stretches the concept even further when he analyzes the six-tone sonority C-D-E-F♯-G-B♭ (equivalent to sc 6-34 [013579]), one of the six-tone subsets of the "seven-tone major-second scale" (i.e., the whole-tone scale on C plus the perfect fifth), as "the projection of two major thirds and two major seconds *above and below* D, and one perfect fifth *below* D."[127] Here again Hanson's ambiguous terminology is confusing. Although this could refer to either one or two major thirds and major seconds above and below D, from its use in other contexts it becomes clear that here it means the projection of one major third above and one major third below D, one major second above and one major second below D, and a perfect fifth below D. A more fundamental problem in the above statement is that Hanson has already picked C, not D, as the starting or generating tone of this sonority. Of course, the choice of C is arbitrary, but it makes no difference which tone is selected; the point is that Hanson has ordered this sonority, as he has every sonority up to this point in the book, on the basis of its projection from a particular generating tone, and he now offers an explanation deriving it from a *different* tone. Subsequently he reinterprets other sonorities in the same cavalier way. If there was previously any consistency to his ordering of sonorities, this effectively vitiates it.

In Chapter 40 Hanson begins to use yet another meaning of the term projection, when he defines the "projection" of a major triad as its nine-tone complement (or, more precisely, the *involution* of its complement), "since it is in fact the *expansion* or projection of the triad to the nine-tone order."[128] This definition is unlike any of the previous ones, all of which refer to processes of expansion rather than to a single complementary sonority. Nevertheless, Hanson continues to use both meanings for the remainder of the book.

There are analogous problems with Hanson's idiosyncratic interval symbols. He clearly establishes the convention of their use in his Chapter 2, where symbols with numerical superscripts (p^2s, and so forth) express the interval analysis (interval vector) of a sonority. Soon, however, he begins to introduce new uses of his symbols: in Chapter 5, to represent a combined projection—for example, p^2+s^2 for the combined projection of two perfect fifths and two major seconds above a tone (as opposed to the interval analysis of that sonority, p^2mns^2, or sc 4-22 [0247]), and p @ n for the projection of two perfect fifths at the interval of a minor third (as opposed to the interval analysis p^2mn^2s, or sc 4-26 [0358]). Later, in Chapter 50 and in the master diagram at the back of the book, Hanson introduces yet more symbols for such "combined" projections: p/n instead of p @ n, and *PMN* to represent the hexad of the *pmn* projection, i.e., the superimposition of the triad upon itself. For example, *PMN* projected from C would be *pmn* on C (C-E-G) plus *pmn* on E (E-G♯-B) plus *pmn* on G (G-B-D), or C-D-E-G-G♯-B, the interval analysis of which would be $p^3m^4n^3s^2d^2t$, or sc 6-31 [014579].

In Chapter 23 Hanson introduces upward and downward arrows as additional projection symbols, so that $\uparrow p^2$ now represents two fifths projected up, and $p^2\downarrow$ two fifths projected down, although his use of the upward arrow is intermittent. To be strictly accurate, Hanson first uses downward arrows in Chapter 5, but only to indicate the involution of an ordinary upward projection. For example, if d^2 is the projection of two minor seconds above a tone, $d^2\downarrow$ is its involution, i.e., two minor seconds below the tone.

Then in Chapter 35 he adds arrows pointing up *and* down to denote projection both above and below a note, as for instance in the formula $\updownarrow m^2 s^2 p\downarrow$, which represents the sonority described four paragraphs previously, the projection of one major third above and one major third below, one major second above and one major second below, and a perfect fifth below a generating tone (sc 6-34 [013579]); compare its interval analysis $p^2 m^4 n^2 s^4 dt^2$. This new symbology is also ambiguous; only from context is it clear that the up-and-down arrow applies to the second interval, s^2, as well as to the first. (The reader is also reminded that $\updownarrow m^2$ means a major third above plus a major third below a given note, not two major thirds above plus two below—although in this case the tones described would be the same.) This employment of the same interval symbols for very different uses is another source of unnecessary confusion in *Harmonic Materials*. While the use of arrows does help to distinguish projection descriptions from interval analyses, Hanson never clearly establishes the distinction, nor does he consistently maintain it. He soon compounds the confusion when he reveals that, even with these new uses of his symbols, there can be several possible representations of sonorities, as when he describes the tetrad C-D♯-E-A (sc 4-18 [0147]) as either $\updownarrow n^2 m^1\uparrow$ or $n^2 + p^1$.[129] He even occasionally uses the same term for two different sonorities, as when he uses M^6 to represent both the six-tone and seven-tone projections of the major third, and does the same with S^6 for the six-tone and seven-tone projections of the major second.[130] In this case Hanson has confused his use of the numerical superscript following capital letters—where it denotes the number of times the capitalized interval is projected—with his use of the superscript following uncapitalized letters—where it denotes the number of occurrences of the interval in the analysis (interval vector). Since these sonority "names" refer to projection rather than to interval analysis, the six-tone projections should have been labelled M^5 and S^5.[131]

In short, projection is the "wild card" in Hanson's theory. Although as a composer he considered it the heart of the theory, in a very real sense he never reconciled it with the rest of his system. The problem with attempting to incorporate the concept of projection into a theory may be that, by its very nature, it describes a compositional process, one that is essentially generative or expansive, rather than theoretical or deductive. Unlike such concepts as interval classes and set classes, projections may not be arranged easily (or perhaps at all) into simple, mutually exclusive categories without duplications or omissions. This cannot be decided, however, until or unless the inconsistencies in Hanson's conceptual structure are resolved.

We can gain another viewpoint on projection by summarizing the above discussion in a brief comparison of Hanson's theory with set theory. With regard to the first of Hanson's stated goals—a systematic classification of all the sonorities contained within the chromatic scale—it seems hard to deny that while Hanson's theory came first, set theory is clearer, more consistent, and (for the most part) easier to utilize and to interpret. The most important differences include the following:

1. The terminology and symbology used in the classic formulations of set theory, such as those by Forte, Straus, and Rahn, are relatively consistent and clearly defined, unlike Hanson's.[132] Set theory's use of integers to represent pitch classes as the elements of a collection makes it far easier to denote and to classify any given sonority, than Hanson's use of alphanumeric symbols to show projection origins—although it must be acknowledged that Hanson's inclusion of each sonority's interval succession, represented as a series of integers (throughout the book and in the master diagram), does allow the derivation of an involution (inversion) very quickly.[133] Similarly, the listing of all sets of a given cardinality in a consistent numerical order and with consistent "set names" is far easier to work with than Hanson's bewildering multiplicity of types of projections and projection symbols. On his final master diagram there are sometimes as many as three different "projection" labels for a sonority, and even here the naming of sonorities is inconsistent. For example, all tetrads, pentads and hexads are represented by projection symbols—except for two isomeric tetrads represented only by their interval analyses, *pmnsdt* (the "all-interval tetrachords" of set theory). Apparently Hanson was unable to find a projection to "explain" them.[134]

2. Set theory's use of normal order and prime form offer a consistent ordering for each and every possible pitch-class collection, and tables such as the "Simplified Set List" given as Appendix 2 in Straus's *Introduction to Post-Tonal Theory* allow any given sonority to be quickly classified and compared to any other sonority of the same cardinality. If one wishes to compare two sets of the same cardinality to find out whether or not they are equivalent, it is a relatively quick and simple matter to represent each tone as an integer, modulo 12 (where C=0, C♯=1, and so forth), to put the first set in ascending numerical order, to compare it with the list of sets to find out the set class to which it belongs, and to do the same for the other. Hanson offers no such method, nor does his master diagram provide one. Since his sonorities are listed in an order based on projection, rather than on any numerical aspect of interval analysis or interval succession, the closest thing to a short way of comparing two sonorities of the same cardinality provided by *Harmonic Materials* is to look through the list of sonorities of that cardinality

in Chapter 50 or in the master diagram, and to attempt to match the interval succession of the given sonorities with that of every sonority and every involution listed, one after the other.

3. Because set theory uses integers to represent pitch classes, deals with inherent properties of integers and of groups, and uses mathematical operations applicable to integers and groups, set theorists have been able to discover or formulate many general rules. Although Hanson clearly discovered a good number of these rules, he was unable to formulate them rigorously, or sometimes even to state them. One such omission has already been discussed: Although Hanson shows in the course of *Harmonic Materials* that all hexads (hexachords) have the same interval analysis (interval vector) as their complements, he never states this as a general rule. Yet it is a commonplace of set theory.[135] Similarly he never states, although he clearly seems to know, the more general rule of which this is an instance, that the arithmetic difference of corresponding vector entries for complementary sets is the same as the difference of the cardinal numbers of the sets (except for ic 6, for which the difference must be divided by two).[136] On pages 351–52 of *Harmonic Materials* he gives almost every specific instance of this rule, but never states the rule itself.

As we have also seen, when Hanson states that the "maverick sonority" (sc 5Z-12) is unique in not being a subset of its complement, he fails to recognize, or at least to mention, that this is also true of all isomeric (Z-related) hexads. Set-theory literature reveals many other such general statements and rules which Hanson, without a rigorous and consistent procedure, did not discover. On the other hand, considering the vastly greater amount of work necessitated by his lack of the tools of set theory (including computers), the many rules and patterns he did discover are all the more impressive. It should also be kept in mind that *Harmonic Materials* was the first and only formulation of Hanson's theory to appear in print. Unlike Babbitt and Forte, he has had no followers extending or improving on his work in subsequent decades, and his work has had no published revisions.

Yet if Hanson's theory is inferior to set theory as a system of classification in all these ways, is there anything that might justify its study and development? Three aspects of Hanson's theory must be considered before consigning it to being purely of historical interest. Two of them—its purported value as a tool of analysis, and its purported value as a compositional tool—are explored in subsequent chapters. There is, however, a third aspect to be considered in regard to his central concept of projection. (Here "projection" is used in its original meaning of a consistent process of expansion of an inter-

val or sonority into progresssively larger sonorities.) Chapters 41
through 47 of *Harmonic Materials* show, for each projection, a list of
related sonorities of increasing cardinality from the basic sonority
to its complement. In Chapter 41, for example, are lists showing the
doad, triad, tetrad, pentad, hexad, heptad, octad, nonad, and decad
for, respectively, the perfect-fifth, minor-second, major-second,
minor-third, major-third, and tritone projections. (Appendix G
shows one of these, the major-second projection.) These "family
trees" reveal a considerable amount about tonal relations for the
composer or the analyst.

For one example of this we may turn to a set-theory concept developed by Forte called the "set complex."[137] Briefly put, the set
complex K around a "nexus set" T (and its complement) is an array
consisting of all set classes of cardinality greater than one and less
than eleven that are either subsets or supersets of either T or its complement. An additional condition is that the cardinality of these set
classes must be different from the cardinality of either T or its complement. (In the 1964 article Forte's set complexes include two-element and ten-element set classes, but in *The Structure of Atonal
Music* Forte eliminates them, although he does not explain why. He
may have come to feel that, since there are only six distinct set
classes for each of these cardinalities, their inclusion would add
nothing significant to distinguish each set complex. Also, it is easy
to find the number of occurrences of each two-element set class from
the interval vector, and each two-element set class would of course
imply its ten-element complement.)

For most nexus sets, K is so large as to be virtually useless, so
Forte defines the "most significant subcomplex" Kh (called K_S in
the 1964 article) as the array consisting of all set classes that are either subsets or supersets of both T *and* its complement. On the next
page is Forte's first example, the subcomplex Kh around sc 5-33 (the
so-called "whole-tone pentachord") and its complement, 7-33. The
format in this diagram is essentially the earlier one used by Forte
in his 1964 article, rather than his later abstract or triangle-shaped
formats as used in *The Structure of Atonal Music*, because the former is more compact and easier to read, and because in 1964 Forte
was still including two-element and ten-element sets in the set
complex.[138] In this diagram the set classes above the horizontal line
are supersets of 5-33, and those below the line are subsets of 7-33.
Complementary set classes are arranged symmetrically above and
below the line; since all the hexachords in this set complex are self-
complementary, they appear both above and below. A set theorist
would expect this diagram, applied to a "free atonal" (i.e., nonse-
rial) piece in which sc 5-33 or 7-33 figured prominently, to show a

	6-35				
	6-34		8-25	9-12	10-6
	6-22		8-24	9-8	10-4
5-33	6-21	7-33	8-21	9-6	10-2
7-33	6-21	5-33	4-21	3-6	2-2
	6-22		4-24	3-8	2-4
	6-34		4-25	3-12	2-6
	6-35				

great deal about the connections between some of the most important sonorities occurring in the work. For example, he would expect to find that many of the hexachords and tetrachords in the diagram are also prominently featured, either melodically or harmonically, throughout the piece. In addition, a set theorist might be interested in such issues as similarity relations among sets of the same cardinality, and invariance of subsets under transposition and inversion. However, these concerns would still apply primarily to questions of unity and connectedness in atonal pieces rather than to tonal relations between sonorities.

While this figure demonstrates inclusion relations among the nexus set and others of greater or lesser cardinality, *Harmonic Materials* shows all of these relations in a way that makes them easier to find for specific sonorities. Although Hanson makes no use of set terminology, all of the information in Forte's diagram, and more, can be found in *Harmonic Materials*. Set class 5-33 can be found in Chapter 9 as the pentad of the major-second projection S^4, produced by superimposing four successive major seconds above C, or C-D-E-F♯-G♯.[139] Hanson goes on to discuss the pentad's subsets: the "triad" C-D-E, the augmented triad C-E-G♯, and the "triad" C-D-F♯ (or sc 3-6 [024], 3-8 [026], and 3-12 [048]). Then he discusses the three types of tetrads: C-D-E-F♯, C-D-E-G♯, and C-E-F♯-A♯ (sc 4-21 [0246], 4-24 [0248], and 4-25 [0268]). In the next chapter, by adding a foreign tone, Hanson constructs the "major-second heptad," C-D-E-F♯-G-G♯-A♯ (sc 7-33 [012468T], which he later shows, in Chapter 41, to be the complement of the S^4 pentad); and in Chapter 35 he analyzes its component hexads, which are of course equivalent to sc 6-21 [023468], 6-22 [012468], 6-34 [013579], and 6-35 [02468T]. The "doads" can be found in the pentad's interval analysis, $m^4s^4t^2$—m, s, and t being equivalent to sc 2-4, 2-2, and 2-6.

All of the above information can be found, more quickly and conveniently (with a little practice), in Hanson's master diagram (see Appendix A). If the diagram is rotated 90° clockwise, the pentads can be found within the second-lowest horizontal block, with the Roman numeral V to its left. They are divided into smaller groups,

according to their predominant interval, by dotted lines running
across the page. In the third such group proceeding downward, the
top row shows S^4 (the sonority under discussion) with interval analysis 040402 and interval succession 2-2-2-2-4. Following the row toward the right, immediately to the right of the staircase-shaped dark
line, are four crosses. These indicate intersections with the columns running downward from the four hexads mentioned above,
showing that this pentad is a subset of each of them. Then, farther to
the right, there are crosses at the intersections with the columns
running downward from the three tetrads mentioned. When those
columns are followed farther downward to the bottommost section,
representing the triads, there are crosses at the intersections with the
rows containing the three triads mentioned; and at the far right of
these rows are crosses indicating the constituent intervals or doads.

In short: With the addition of the complements of the above sets,
which can also be found easily in the master diagram, *Harmonic
Materials* furnishes all the information about the relationship of
sonorities contained in Forte's set-complex diagram—and more;
using either the master diagram or Chapters 41 through 47, it is possible to find all tonal relations for any sonority. It is true that Forte
includes, as an appendix to *The Structure of Atonal Music*, a list of
all Kh subcomplexes for every set class with four to six elements,
and their complements;[140] but a composer or theorist looking for the
sonorities that are related to a given sonority would find this information much more easily in *Harmonic Materials*. To use
Forte's appendix, it is necessary to convert the tones of a sonority to
integers, find the prime form for the set (either by trial-and-error or
by referring to Straus's "Simplified Set List"), look up the set name
in Forte's set list, look up the subcomplex for that set in the appendix,
go back to the set list to look up each related set, then convert each set
back to integers and then, after a reverse transposition, to pitch
classes. Also, Forte excludes all sets of cardinalities two and three
and their complements, eliminating relevant information that is
included in *Harmonic Materials*.

More significantly, Hanson's "family trees" of projections reveal levels of information beyond those of Forte's diagram—relations and degrees of similarity that are intuitively obvious to musicians but are not demonstrable by means of set-class theory. For example, Forte's diagram simply shows that sc 6-21, 6-22, 6-34 and 6-35
are all supersets of 5-33 and subsets of 7-33; but Chapter 41 of
Harmonic Materials also shows that sc 6-35 in particular, the whole-
tone scale, has a uniquely close relationship with sc 5-33. Of the four
hexads only 6-35 is, like 5-33, a member of what may be called the
pure major-second projection (that is, they can both be produced

purely by superimposing major seconds), and only 6-35 contains
nothing but the same three intervals—major third, major second,
and tritone—and in the same relative proportions as the pentad.
This special connection, which would be clear to any musician, is
not to be found in the canons of set-class theory; the ordinal second
half of each Forte set-class name reveals no correspondences except
between complementary set classes. For example, 5-33 corresponds
closely to 7-33, but 6-33 has no special relation to either. Since all the
five-tone subsets of 6-35 are transpositions of each other, there are no
other pentachords in such a close relationship with 5-33.[141] Thus,
Hanson's projection charts show degrees of interrelation not only
for each sonority and its complement, but for all of the related
sonorities of other cardinalities.

More recently, of course, there have appeared set-theoretical
studies by writers such as John Rahn, David Lewin, Marcus Castrén, and Ian Quinn, on the subject of similarity relations, that cover
some of the same ground that Hanson did. In particular, similarity
measures of total subset content, such as Rahn's ATMEMB, Lewin's
REL, and Castrén's RECREL, appear to yield results remarkably
"similar" to Hanson's.[142] Naturally there are significant differences; the most significant by far is that these measures produce
quantitative, comparable results, which Hanson never sought to do.
But what Hanson's "family trees" offer is a direct representation of
certain musical perceptions, the kind of intuitive truths and musical meanings to which all theorists must appeal, explicitly or implicitly, as the ultimate standard for the validity of their models.[143]
Even if the concept of projection needs refinement and revision, it
may carry more musical meaning than do many similarity
measures. Unlike set theorists such as Forte and Schmalfeldt,
whose primary interest in pitch-class sets and their relations is in
their functions of unifying and establishing "motivic" connections
among sections of an atonal work, Hanson's primary interest lies
in the potentialities of the *a priori* relations between the sonorities
themselves, as the raw materials of composition. As he puts it, he is
"more concerned with a study of the *material* of the art and less with
the *manner* of its use, although the two can never be separated."[144]
His treatment of the subject naturally reflects his own interests, but
for those with similar interests, his theory may reveal more than
can be found elsewhere. None of this is to suggest, of course, that
Hanson's theory could or should replace set theory, but simply that,
although projection may be a "wild card"—indeed, perhaps precisely for that reason—his unique approach may reveal aspects of
tonal relations that are as yet unexplored by set theorists.[145]

In any case, one thing cannot be denied: that Hanson was the first to discover, describe, and calculate many of the most fundamental concepts and conclusions of set theory. It is therefore all the more surprising how little credit he has received for this priority. We may well speculate about why this is so, and why Hanson's theory has remained virtually without influence, unknown, and unexplored—despite its having received half a dozen reviews in leading journals when it appeared, most of them positive, including a highly favorable review from Nicolas Slonimsky, who was himself the author of a well-known book on interval relationships.[146]

For those intrepid souls who have actually glanced through *Harmonic Materials,* its arcane terminology may have been enough of an obstacle to keep them from going farther. But few have gone even that far, which suggests that other factors are involved. One is that Hanson was based for forty years in Rochester, at a time when the Eastman School's theory faculty was less prominent nationally than it has been since his retirement. More to the point, as a composer who was not especially interested in theory (other than his own), he seems to have been, and to have kept himself, intellectually isolated from what was going on in Ivy League schools, especially Princeton and Yale, where set theory began. As an example, in 1978 he said, in regard to the arithmetical rule relating the interval vectors of sonorities and their complements, that as far as he knew no other theorist had ever made that point, "and that's why the Yale boys are so mad at me, because they should've done that."[147] This strongly suggests that, as late as five years after the appearance of Forte's *The Structure of Atonal Music,* Hanson remained, if not entirely unaware of the growing body of work in set theory, at least ignorant of some of its most basic formulations.

To this we must add several other factors, such as Hanson's lack of a reputation as a theorist, and his lack of any interest in gaining such a reputation. There is also the inescapable fact that for most of the latter half of the twentieth century, American Romantic composers were largely ignored by American scholars and critics. Had Elliott Carter, for instance, written *Harmonic Materials*, it would surely have been read and discussed by many more theorists. As Jonathan Bernard suggests in his article on the history of the pitch-class set concept, the very fact of Hanson's name, "indelibly associated with compositional conservatism," has probably dissuaded many scholars from bothering to look at his book.[148] Ironically, Bernard's article includes one of the most thorough discussions of *Harmonic Materials* to appear in forty years, and is one of the few to give Hanson credit for first presenting many of the concepts to be found in set-class theory, yet even this article takes a dismissive attitude toward Hanson because of his compositional orientation, with liberal use of phrases like "old-fashioned," "reactionary," and "clinging desperately to the past"—as though, even if these labels were true of Hanson as a composer, they would somehow detract from the originality and significance of his theoretical work. Anticipating such comments, Hanson had written in his unpublished autobiography:

> I am, in my own composition, essentially a traditionalist. I do not believe that this is a contradiction or an inconsistency. A composer may . . . look both forward experimentally toward the future and backward with appreciation and understanding, to the past. The theorist, in my opinion, should do the same.[149]

It is also rather ironic that Bernard criticizes *Harmonic Materials* for its lack of reference to the work of other theorists; it must be admitted that at least some of the obscurity of Hanson's theory is due to reluctance on the part of set theorists, even the few who were familiar with his work, to give Hanson any credit at all, much less credit for being first in many ways. In a scholarly field such as music theory, where citations in bibliographies and footnotes are ubiquitous, it is remarkable how few writers have acknowledged his work or its priority, even granting the many differences in approaches and methods. In Allen Forte's first article on set-class theory, for example, *Harmonic Materials* was included in the Bibliography, but Hanson was otherwise mentioned only in two rather dismissive footnotes. In the first, Forte rejected Hanson's ordering of interval analyses (interval vectors) as being "biased in favor of triadic tonality"—which is inaccurate, although it makes a valid point— and also rejected Hanson's count of sonorities as incorrect, because Hanson lists all isomeric twins and quartets (Z-related sets) separately, while Forte considered Z-related sets as equivalent or isomorphic.[150] But Hanson's classification has ultimately proved to be more valid. Other theorists such as John Clough objected to Forte's use of the interval vector as the standard of equivalence, citing compelling reasons why only sets that were related by transposition and/or inversion should be considered equivalent; and after arguing unconvincingly against this conception, Forte did eventually accept it when he revised and expanded his theory. But this was thirteen years after Hanson had clearly and consistently defined equivalence on the same basis, and had classified "isomeric twins" as nonequivalent, in *Harmonic Materials*.[151]

Despite this, Forte did not retract his earlier criticism of Hanson, nor give Hanson credit for having arrived at the concept of Z-relations first. Instead he credited David Lewin's 1960 article, and most set theorists after him have followed suit.[152] Forte also gave Lewin credit for first revealing several unusual properties of sc 5-Z12 (the "maverick sonority"), and for first discussing (along with Milton Babbitt) the arithmetic relationship between the interval vectors of complementary sets; but Hanson had already discussed both of these subjects in *Harmonic Materials*.[153] It is true that Lewin's article appeared within a few weeks of *Harmonic Materials*, but scholars with any experience of publication know that as a rule, a book takes much longer to appear in print than a journal article. Logically, then, even discounting Hanson's assertion in his Preface that he had been working on the theory for "over a quarter-century," a theorist would have had to presume that Hanson had arrived at the concept and put it into words earlier.[154] Thus George Perle credits Hanson and Lewin equally for the concept of the Z-relation, and Janet Schmalfeldt acknowledges that Hanson "may have been the first" to describe and to identify the Z-related sonorities.[155]

On the other hand Schmalfeldt, while acknowledging *Harmonic Materials* as "an important breakthrough," dismisses it abruptly with a few ambiguous comments, which suggest misleadingly that, unlike Forte, Hanson was not able to accurately deal with or distinguish Z-related sonorities.[156] As shown above, this is not only untrue, it is the opposite of the truth: it was Forte who treated Z-related sets as equivalent in his first set-theory article, and criticized Hanson for an incorrect count of sonorities because Hanson counted Z-related sets as distinct. Nor is this the only invalid criticism that Schmalfeldt makes of *Harmonic Materials*, with the effect of making set theory appear unequivocally superior. While she acknowledges that Chapter 49 and the foldout diagram are "an impressive first attempt" to indicate the web of potential inclusion relations, she also says that Hanson "was not prepared . . . to pursue" the relations of sonorities of different cardinality. She claims that in relation to any sonority of cardinality n the diagram shows only the related sonorities of cardinality $n+1$ and $n-1$, but as shown above, this is not true; indeed, she implicitly contradicts this claim immediately by adding that one has to trace higher- or lower-cardinality sonorities through the intervening sonorities, which is true.[157]

The second footnote to mention Hanson in Forte's 1964 article criticized what Forte called two errors on Hanson's part, but while one of those errors is real—Hanson's neglecting to refer to the hexachords in regard to the uniqueness of the "maverick sonority"—the other is not: Forte criticized Hanson's assertion that the "maverick sonority" is not a part (subset) of its complement as incorrect, and yet any trained theorist can check Hanson's assertion and see that in fact it is correct. Forte's objection to it was based on his having devised an arbitrary mapping of this pentachord onto its complement, a mapping that has no musical meaning.[158] Mention of this mapping was omitted from *The Structure of Atonal Music*; also omitted, however, was any mention of Hanson at all. Forte's contribution to set theory is unquestionably both seminal and immense, and none of the above is meant to imply in any way that he did not develop much of it himself. Even so, however, and even if he had developed the entire theory himself before reading *Harmonic Materials*, it would be reasonable to expect him to have acknowledged, at least, that much of what he was presenting was either similar or identical to what Hanson had already presented. His failure to do so is rather surprising, and one cannot help wondering whether Hanson's theory would have had quite a different reception and history if Forte had acknowledged its priority.

Since its publication, the acknowledgments of Hanson's work have remained few. If *Harmonic Materials* is mentioned, it is usually in a brief citation as part of a long list.[159] However, this is unfair both to Hanson and to ourselves. Despite the flaws in his presentation and the idiosyncrasies of his terminology, some of Hanson's concepts—such as projection, aspects of inversional symmetry, and the hierarchical web of related sonorities to be found between set classes and their complements—indicate aspects of tonal relations that have yet to be thoroughly explored in set theory. For this reason, if for no other, Hanson's theory may be worth further study and development.

THE QUESTION OF AUTHORSHIP

There is one more subject that needs to be discussed before we proceed further. While researching this book, I encountered rumors among theorists, at the Eastman School of Music and elsewhere, to the effect that either Howard Hanson did not write *Harmonic Materials*, or he did not write it alone. Research has uncovered a single name as the putative author or co-author, that of Robert V. Sutton, who was born in 1923. After receiving a B.M. from the University of Alabama, and teaching theory and cello at the University of Montana, Sutton earned M.M. and Ph.D. degrees from the Eastman School of Music. He taught theory and composition there from 1955 to 1973, during which time he often used the Hanson theory—as we shall continue to call it, at least for now—in doctoral-level courses.

In the late 1960s, after Hanson had retired, Sutton headed an association devoted to improving working conditions for faculty. A popular teacher, he apparently expected to be given chairmanship of the theory department but, possibly because of his "unionizing" activities, he was passed over, and soon left the Eastman School. From 1973 to 1988 he taught at the University of Massachusetts at Amherst, serving as chair of the Department of Music and Dance for three years, and continuing to teach the Hanson theory to his classes there. He was a member of the National Council of the College Music Society and served the Music Teachers National Association in a number of capacities, eventually becoming its president from 1979 to 1981. Early in 1986 he suffered a severe heart attack from which he never fully recovered. He died in 1994.[160]

The problem with the rumors about Sutton having devised, or having made a significant contribution to, the theory is that there is no factual information to confirm them, while there is a considerable amount of information to contradict them. Besides Hanson's own words about the years he spent developing the theory, a number of his students have recalled studying the theory with him before Sutton arrived at the Eastman School.[161] In the Acknowledgments section of *Harmonic Materials*, Hanson does thank Sutton, as one of his "colleagues of the Eastman School of Music . . . for valuable criticism," along with Wayne Barlow, Allen Irvine McHose, Charles Riker, and Herbert Inch (who had moved to Hunter College). But the picture that emerges from the recollections of former students and colleagues who knew both Hanson and Sutton, some of whom are still on the faculty of the Eastman School, is the common one of an author in academia who has discussed his new ideas with friends and colleagues, and has asked them to read and critique his manuscript before submitting it for publication. Like the other Eastman School colleagues whom Hanson mentions, Sutton probably contributed some suggestions in the final stages of the theory or the book. But there is no evidence to suggest that his contributions went beyond that.

More importantly, there is Sutton's own testimony. Six years after Hanson's death, Sutton published an article about the theory.[162] Certainly at this point, if he had been the author or co-author, he could have taken credit for *Harmonic Materials*; Hanson was dead and his reputation had diminished too far to suffer from any revelations concerning such an obscure book. But instead the article focuses on the chronological priority of Hanson's theory in relation to set theory. According to his own account, Sutton was first exposed to Hanson's theory as a graduate student in the 1948–49 school year, at one of the informal seminars that Hanson would hold with graduate students and teachers to discuss the theory. In 1955, with "Hanson's book . . . complete in typescript," Sutton began to use it as a textbook in a doctoral-level course, as did other members of the theory and composition faculty. This is his only claim to any connection with the theory; he takes no credit for any part of it. Of course it is possible that Sutton simply wished to get the credit for priority at second hand, and to remain behind the scenes, so to speak—but this raises the question of why he would have bothered to maintain the subterfuge. Only a week before his incapacitating heart attack, he wrote a letter to Hanson's widow expressing his intention to write another article on the chronological context of Hanson's theory, in which he referred to his years of "teaching from the manuscript" of the book, and his conviction that "not nearly enough credit [was] being given to Dr. Hanson."[163]

When I attempted to track down the sources and possible factual bases for this rumor, an interesting fact emerged: most of those from whom I heard it did not know Hanson personally, and none of them knew him well. A typical comment, from a set theorist at the Eastman School who had known Hanson only slightly, was that Hanson's music does not show the intellectual power or interest necessary to conceive and work out a book as ambitious as *Harmonic Materials*—that Hanson was not a "big brain"—and that therefore he must have had help.

The consensus among most of his former students and colleagues, on the other hand, is that Hanson was extremely intelligent, and (as one of them put it) "too much of a gentleman not to share credit" if it was due. But in addition to the evidence already cited, Hanson's other writings seem clearly to refute the contention that he was not intelligent enough to have produced the theory himself, a contention which has had a vogue primarily among set theorists. Certainly it is illogical to criticize the theory for its flaws, attributing them to Hanson's own aesthetic predilections, and then proceed to deny his authorship. There would also remain the question of why someone who considered himself a composer, not a theorist, would bother to spend the time and effort necessary for such an elaborate fabrication, in order to attain some hypothetical glory in a field in which he had little or no interest.

There is one further body of evidence to be weighed in this matter, and it is a massive one: the thousands of pages of sketches and calculations of intervals and projections for the theory that Hanson left behind.[164] A large number of them appear on the pages of music notebooks, and in the margin or on the verso of sheets of music paper devoted to compositions, going back at least to the 1940s. Many more are on loose sheets of music or ledger paper in a wide variety of sizes, often wrapped around sheets devoted to other purposes.

Study of these sketches also reveals that the symbols used to represent interval classes in the theory went through at least three stages, and possibly more. The earliest one was a system in which *a* represented perfect fifths and fourths, *b* represented major and minor thirds, *c* represented major seconds, *d* minor seconds, and *e* tritones. (The use of a single symbol to represent all thirds will seem absurd to a modern theorist, but it may reflect an earlier stage of Hanson's ideas in which, still thinking in more traditional terms, he did not distinguish absolutely between major and minor thirds.)[165] This was followed by a revision in which *B* stood for major thirds and *b* for minor thirds, a clear improvement that had been made by the time of the sketches for the Concerto for Piano and Orchestra, which was completed in 1948.[166] Finally, perhaps after the initial plans for publication in 1952 had been abandoned, Hanson changed to the final symbology.

Interestingly enough, for at least a short time he considered using integers to represent interval classes. In a box containing miscellaneous material that seems to be from different periods—including sketches for *Merry Mount*, the *Sinfonia Sacra*, and the *Elegy*, and dozens of sheets of music paper using the first- and second-stage symbols, with painstaking calculations of different interval successions and interval analyses—there are several sheets that use integers instead, on one of which is a tabular column that reads, "m2=1, M2[=]2, m3=3, M3=4, P4=5, aug4=6."[167] While this use of integers to express interval classes was clearly an intermediate stage of work on the theory, it is impossible to say when Hanson made this experiment, or why he abandoned it. It does raise some provocative speculations. Had Hanson persisted with this notation, the last fifty years of music theory might have been quite different.

In any case, the sheer amount of material related to the theory, in three or four different phases, of which a significant proportion can be dated, seems to indicate conclusively that even if Hanson had some help in certain details of the theory or of its presentation, he developed the theory himself, painstakingly and without help of computing machines or assistants, over a period of many years—precisely as he claimed.

Chapter 5

The Theory Considered
as a Method of Analysis

At the end of the Preface to *Harmonic Materials*, Hanson asserts that a student who masters his theory "will have at his disposal an analytical technic which will enable him to analyze factually any passage or phrase written in the twelve-tone equally tempered scale" (p. xi). Throughout the book he quotes and analyzes excerpts from various pieces. A handful of these are from the nineteenth century, and all the rest are from the twentieth; of the latter, the great majority are from tonal and what might be called tonally centric or "pantonal" pieces, such as Stravinsky's *Petrushka, Symphony of Psalms* and Symphony in C, and two pieces by Messaien. A few are from pieces usually considered "freely atonal," such as Schoenberg's Five Pieces for Orchestra, Opus 16, and two of Bartók's String Quartets. Only one example, the beginning of Berg's *Lyrische Suite*, is from a dodecaphonic piece. In general, each musical example is short—usually two measures—and Hanson's analysis consists of treating every note in the example as part of a single sonority, which the excerpt has been chosen to illustrate.

A brief look at one of Hanson's examples will illustrate certain unique strengths of his method. He quotes an excerpt from the first movement of Stravinsky's *Symphony of Psalms,* where the chorus first sings. See Example 5.1.[168]

Example 5.1   Stravinsky, *Symphony of Psalms,* I, rehearsal 4

The configuration upon which this passage is based (E-F-G-G♯-A♯-B-C♯-D, sc 8-28 [0134679T]), which had been used by earlier Russian composers such as Stravinsky's teacher Rimsky-Korsakov, is usually called the octatonic scale or collection, and explained as an "artificial" scale consisting of alternating whole tones and semitones. Some writers derive it from the combination of two symmetrical partitionings of the chromatic scale, i.e., diminished seventh chords.[169] Hanson, however, derives this sonority, as E-F-G-G♯-B♭-B-D♭-D, from the octad of the minor-third projection, C. N^3, with interval analysis $p^4m^4n^8s^4d^4t^4$.[170] Since the first eight tones of the minor-third projection on E would be E-G-B♭-D♭ plus B-D-F-G♯ (taking the fifth above the starting tone as the first "foreign" tone), this sonority could also be considered the combination of two diminished seventh chords. However, it should be remembered that in Hanson's system the diminished sevenths are not derived by reduction (the partitioning of an eight-note collection into two four-note collections) but by generation (the projection of a basic interval), and thus they imply specific interrelationships among the basic interval, the octad, and all the members of the minor-third "family tree" in between. The passage is saturated with melodic minor thirds: the combined oboe/English horn line below the melody consists of alternating pairs of minor thirds (as does the cello/double bass line that appears below this material when it returns at rehearsal 7), and the arpeggiated bassoon line in the bass clef contains three minor thirds in each measure. Hanson would analyze the bassoon line alone as N^5, the six-tone projection of the minor third, which is of course a subset of C. N^3.[171] Since Stravinsky himself has said that "sequences of two minor thirds joined by a major third" were "the root idea of the whole work,"[172] Hanson's analysis of this excerpt, deriving it from a tonal complex saturated with minor thirds, offers a plausible and perhaps deeper alternative to the usual "octatonic collection" derivation.

But other excerpts in the book, such as Example 5.2, reveal limitations in his method of analysis. Hanson presents this excerpt, the opening of the Coronation Scene from *Boris Godunov*, as an illustration of the *pmn*-tritone projection, i.e., the superimposition of tritones above each tone of a major (or minor) triad, or equivalently, the superimposition of one major (or minor) triad above another one at the interval of a tritone.[173] He analyzes this sonority as an A♭ major triad with a superimposed D major triad, or A♭-A-C-D-E♭-F♯.[174]

Example 5.2   Mussorgsky, *Boris Godunov*, Act I Scene 2

Hanson's analysis includes all the tones and intervals present in the excerpt, and provides an interesting and perhaps even plausible analysis of its overall harmonic basis, but it could well be objected that this does not acknowledge as significant something that is clearly visible and audible to any musician: the alternation of two dominant seventh chords a tritone apart. This is significant because the six tones are never heard simultaneously, only as two alternating seventh chords, and also because part of the inherent interest of such an alternation for a composer is that half the tones of each chord are common tones. By ignoring the repetitions of the C-G♭ (or C-F♯) tritone because they constitute "doublings," Hanson could be said to have ignored an important feature of Mussorgsky's compositional choice. It might also be considered a limitation of such an analysis that, even if it is valid, it is on an extremely small scale, and says nothing about the excerpt's relation to the rest of the Coronation Scene or the rest of the opera. (In this particular case, the alternation occurs in only one other place—in Boris's death scene in Act IV.)

Many of Hanson's other analyses also lump together alternating chords into a single hypothetical sonority, and many of them likewise ignore harmonic entities, such as triads, that seem to be clearly implied or stated by the composer. In the same chapter he similarly analyzes analogous passages from Stravinsky's *Petrushka* ("Petrushka's Curses" in Tableau II, usually considered either "bitonal" in F♯ and C, or an octatonic subset) and from Britten's *Les Illuminations* (the opening "Fanfare"), and elsewhere he

similarly treats analogous passages in Debussy's *Pelléas et Mélisande,* Respighi's *Pini di Roma,* and Holst's *The Hymn of
Jesus.*[175] On the other hand, as the following chapters will show, the
alternation of two chords often occurs in Hanson's own works, and
his sketches make clear that in at least a significant proportion of
these cases he regarded both chords as halves of a single sonority.
But he offers no evidence that such an analysis is equally valid for
the music of other composers.

Another problem with Hanson's approach can be seen in his
analysis of the excerpt shown in Example 5.3.[176] Although he again
considers both halves of each measure as halves of a single
sonority, rather than alternating broken chords (i.e., E minor followed by G♯ minor, with a C♯ passing tone), such an analysis is considerably more plausible in this case, because the E minor and G♯
minor harmonies sounded together are an important structural
component of this movement, as for instance in measures 22
through 24, and 45 through 49.

Example 5.3   Holst, *The Planets,* "Neptune, the Mystic"

Hanson goes further, however. Instead of considering the C♯ in
the bass clef in measure 1 and the C♯ in the treble clef in measure 2 as
passing tones, he includes them in his hypothetical sonority, which
thus becomes "the complete projection of the triad *pmn* in involution," i.e., projecting downward from D♯, the triad D♯-B-G♯ plus B-G-
E plus G♯-E-C♯, or (arranged upward) C♯-D♯-E-G-G♯-B (sc 6-31
[014579]). Hanson takes a downward projection because, having
taken the major triad as the characteristic form of *pmn*, he must
therefore consider the minor triad as *pmn* in involution (inversion).[177] This "six-tone scale," with interval succession 2-1-3-1-3-2,
is thus the involution of his "six-tone major-triad projection," i.e.,
C-E-G plus E-G♯-B plus G-B-D, or C-D-E-G-G♯-B, with interval
succession 2-2-3-1-3-1 (or, beginning on D, 2-3-1-3-1-2). (Set theory,
on the contrary, takes the minor triad [037] as the paradigmatic or
"prime" form of sc 3-11, because it is more compact than the major
triad: the smaller interval comes first, three semitones rather than
four.) In any case, what this brief excerpt ignores is that except for
this two-measure theme and two recurrences of it, the combined or

alternating E minor and G♯ minor triads appear throughout this movement without a C♯.

This also indicates a broader problem with "reductionist" methods of analysis, such as Hanson's, that include every note of an arbitrarily selected fragment of music. All traditionally tonal music implicitly contains a hierarchy of pitch classes with four distinct levels. In the key of C major, for example, C has a unique primacy. On a slightly lower level of importance are E and G, the other tones of the C major triad; below them are the other four notes of the C major diatonic scale, and below these are the other five tones of the chromatic scale. To ignore this hierarchy in an analysis, and to treat every tone as a part—an equally important part—of the sonority, is to preclude the possibility of harmonic motion, of nonharmonic tones, of dissonance, of resolution, and of any sort of modulation (in the traditional sense). This is problematic for the analysis of many "free atonal" works, as others have noted, but it is even more so for the analysis of tonal music, which is inconceivable without most, if not all, of the above devices. Even Ravel's *Bolero,* perhaps the only tonal piece in the standard repertoire that eschews virtually any melodic or harmonic change, introduces a climactic modulation from C up to E shortly before the end. In addition, the strict application of such a method would make it virtually impossible to acknowledge that a composer has varied a melody slightly by altering several pitches, while preserving a recognizable contour— a fundamental feature of music for hundreds or thousands of years—since altering even a single note by so much as a semitone changes the sonority to a different one.[178]

Such a procedure might seem almost as unwarranted as analyzing a V⁷-I cadence in C major as the six-tone sonority C-D-E-F-G-B, but Hanson goes almost that far when he quotes the excerpt from *Petrushka* given as Example 5.4.[179]

Example 5.4   Stravinsky, *Petrushka,* Second Tableau

Hanson analyzes this as "the six-tone scale formed by the simultaneous projection of three perfect fifths and three minor thirds," i.e., F♯-C♯-G♯-D♯ plus F♯-A-B♯-D♯. He immediately adds that

the excerpt "can, of course, also be analyzed as a dominant ninth in C♯ minor followed by the tonic"; but he gives no reason why his first analysis should be considered to have equal, much less greater, validity than this alternative.

Hanson does not seem to have made up his mind about this issue. At one point, he states clearly:

> In detailed analysis it seems generally wise to analyze every note in a passage regardless of its relative importance, rather than dismissing certain notes as "nonharmonic" or "unessential" tones, for all tones in a passage are important, even though they may be only appoggiaturas or some other form of ornamentation.[180]

Yet he immediately goes on to add, "Occasionally, however, the exclusion of such 'unessential' tones seems obvious," and adduces an example from the Debussy Prelude "Voiles" in which all notes are part of the whole-tone scale beginning on C, except for a thirty-second-note G and a thirty-second-note D♭. "Since both of these notes were quite obviously conceived as passing tones, it would seem unrealistic to analyze them as integral parts of the tonal complex." This would be difficult to dispute, but the question inevitably arises: On what basis—other than an *a priori* decision that the whole-tone scale is the operative sonority—has Hanson decided that the Debussy example constitutes an allowable exception to his general rule, but the Holst example does not? Hanson never explains the basis for his distinction.[181]

A final deficiency of Hanson's analytic method, for those who demand from a musical theory a scope that embraces the larger aspects of a composition such as structure, unity, and long-range melodic or harmonic motion, is that it is concerned only with small-scale events. Nowhere in *Harmonic Materials* is there a view from a wider perspective than that shown in the above examples, nor is there any consideration of the relative structural importance of tones, lines, or sonorities. To those accustomed to theories that purport to explain the longer-range (or "middleground" and "background") aspects of a composition, such as Schenkerian analysis, or set-class theory as applied by Allen Forte to *The Rite of Spring* and by Janet Schmalfeldt to *Wozzeck*, Hanson's refusal to deal with anything beyond the smallest units of harmony or melody would seem disappointingly limited.[182] The longest analysis in *Harmonic Materials*, dealing with the first twenty-seven measures of Roy Harris's Symphony no. 3, does no more than split up Harris's long melody—which, taken as a single sonority, includes all twelve tones—into smaller segments, each of which is then "analyzed" for the sonority it represents. Even here, there is no coherent or consistent explanation of the rationale behind Hanson's choices of segmentation. In set-theory literature there are many instances of analyses where segmentation choices can be, and have been, disputed. It is often difficult, if not impossible, to reach a consensus on how to determine the boundaries beyond which a set cannot plausibly be inferred, or on whether such factors as registral associations, rhythmic parallels, or durational or timbral connections can be said to link tones that are separated by time or pitch space.[183] Hanson offers no insights into these questions, giving the impression that his own choices are entirely *ad hoc* and arbitrary. No account is taken in his analysis of the Harris excerpt of any larger-scale considerations, such as the influence of style or of a tonal hierarchy—nothing beyond the observation, which would be obvious to anyone familiar with the excerpt, that when it begins it is basically G-centric, and when it ends it is basically B-centric.[184] Nor do Hanson's analyses reveal any insights into the compositional methods or precompositional intentions of the composers whose works are analyzed.[185]

Yet it is evident from his choice of examples, and from what we shall see in the following chapters, that small-scale analysis is the only analysis that interests Hanson—indeed, that it apparently comprises the extent to which he finds analysis to be relevant or useful. As he says in his Preface, *Harmonic Materials* and the entire theory it contains is intended only as a compendium, a dictionary or thesaurus of sounds, "in much the same way that a dictionary or thesaurus serves the author," but does not furnish grammar, logic, or structure.[186] Hanson was, after all, a composer and not a theorist. It could also be said with some accuracy that most post-tonal analyses deal with similarly short time spans.

Still, it is natural for a theorist to wonder: What, according to Hanson, is to determine the larger-scale formal and structural aspects of a piece of music, on either a conscious or unconscious level? As we shall see, Hanson seems to feel, like Debussy and others before him, that these should be determined by the composer's "ear," his intuitive sense of proportion and balance—although Hanson reluctantly makes allowances for those who wish to consciously impose an *a priori* tonal ordering, such as some type of serialism, on their composition. For his own music—with the partial exception of the two special pieces to be discussed in the next chapter—the remainder of this book will show that to a significant extent, Hanson was content to let the traditional forms and progressions that he had inherited and adapted for himself determine the larger-scale movement and structure of his music. Although the usefulness of his theory as a tool of analysis may thus be limited, it should be borne in mind that he only claimed that it could analyze any passage or phrase written using the chromatic collection, not that it was capable of analyzing an entire movement or piece; and that, as was noted at the end of the last chapter, his concern in *Harmonic Materials* was with "the *material* of the art" and not with "the *manner* of its use."

Chapter 6

The Two Demonstration Pieces

Hanson wrote two pieces that were intended, at least in part, to demonstrate aspects of his theory. The first of these was *For the First Time,* a suite in twelve movements subtitled "Twelve Impressions in a Child's Day." Later in life Hanson said of this work, "it was really almost an exposition of my harmonic theories."[187] As he explains in his notes and in his recorded oral analysis of the piece, he had two primary goals in writing it: the first was to tell "a very simple and unsophisticated story in music through a series of movements"; the second, to utilize a different and appropriate "'chemical mixture' of tones" for each movement from the possibilities presented in *Harmonic Materials.*[188] He goes on to give an extremely brief and simplified disquisition on the six basic intervals (i.e., interval classes), and then he shows—and on the recorded analysis, his orchestra plays—the sonority that forms the basis of each movement. Six of the twelve movements are based on sonorities with a preponderance of a single interval. For example, "Bells" is based on the first five tones of the perfect-fifth projection, C-G-D-A-E. The other six movements are based on more complex and "impure" sonorities that combine various intervals. For example, "Deep Forest" is based on the projection of *pmn* (the major triad) at the tritone, or C-E-G plus F♯-A♯-C♯. In short, Hanson intended the piece to serve both as an entertainment and as an embodiment and demonstration of his theory. Table 6.1 shows the title of each movement and the sonority on which it is based. (Alternative terms used

Table 6.1
For the First Time: **Harmonic Analysis by Movement**

	movement title	Hanson term	equivalent set class
I.	Bells	P^4	5-35 [02479]
II.	Tamara and Peter Bolshoi (Two playful Irish terrier puppies with Russian names)	D^6	7-1 [0123456]
III.	The Deserted House	T^3 (p^2/t)*	6-7 [012678]
IV.	The Eccentric Clock	C. p^2s †	9-9 [01235678T]
V.	Deep Forest	pmn/t	6-30 [013679]
VI.	Clowns	C. M^3	9-12 [01245689T]
VII.	Dance ‡	*PNS* (*pmn/s*)	6-33 [023579]
VIII.	Serious Conversations	*PMN*	6-31 [014579]
IX.	Kikimora	*NSD* (s^3d^3)	6-2 [012346]
X.	Mist	S^6 *	6-35 [02468T]
XI.	Fireworks	N^5 inv.	6-27 [013469]
XII.	Dreams ‡	*pns/s*	5-23 [02357]

*Hanson's names for the sonorities used in "The Deserted House" and "Mist" are actually misnomers. Although the "T^3" sonority only contains three tritones (the other three being "foreign tones"), it is the sonority produced by a fivefold tritone projection, and thus by analogy to P^5 and the other fivefold interval projections, its correct name should be T^5. Similarly, the correct name for the "S^6" sonority should be S^5, since it is the sonority produced by projecting five major seconds (i.e., the whole-tone scale). See the discussion of Hanson's inconsistent symbology in the fourth chapter of this book.

†In his Foreword, liner notes and oral analysis, Hanson calls this "the three-tone chord CEF♯ 'projected' at the interval 'p' to a ten-tone combination." This is misleading; the projection used in this piece (C-E-F♯, G-B-C♯, D-F♯-G♯, A) is only a nine-tone sonority, because F♯ occurs twice.

‡Pencilled notations on the holograph of the full score indicate that the seventh movement was originally, or temporarily, entitled "Polka," and that the twelfth movement was originally, or temporarily, entitled "Lullaby."

by Hanson follow his primary ones in parentheses. In this table, numerical superscripts refer to projections, not to interval analysis. As explained in the previous chapter, the prefix "C." before a sonority name denotes the complement of that sonority. The term "inv." means that Hanson has used the involution of the sonority as it is presented in *Harmonic Materials.*)

For the First Time exists in two versions, one for piano solo and one for orchestra. The work has a curious history. On the one hand, the piano version seems to be a later transcription of the orchestral version; the orchestral version was published in 1963 and the piano version in 1970. James E. Perone calls the piano version "Hanson's piano reduction of" the orchestral version.[189] This view is supported by an interesting anomaly. In measure 4 of the second movement, "Tamara and Peter Bolshoi," the notes of the treble line in the piano version are a whole tone higher than those in the orchestral version. (See Examples 6.1A and 6.1B.) This is the only difference between the two versions in the entire work, other than the occasional slight differences in register and doubling that are inevitably found between orchestral and piano arrangements of the same material.

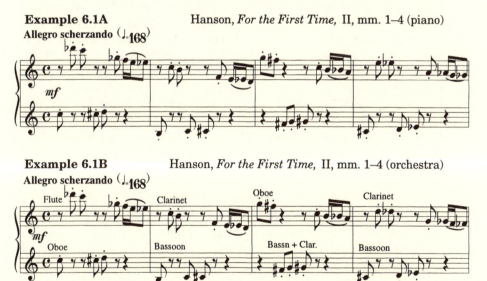

Example 6.1A   Hanson, *For the First Time,* II, mm. 1–4 (piano)

Example 6.1B   Hanson, *For the First Time,* II, mm. 1–4 (orchestra)

In both versions, measure 2 is an exact transposition of measure 1, forming a sequence; and in the orchestral version, measure 4 is also a transposition. Such sequential passages are a prominent feature of this movement: measure 7 is a transposition of measure 6, and measures 20 through 21 are a transposition of measures 8 through 9 (except for two notes on the downbeat of measure 8 that are missing in measure 20). In the piano version, however, measure 4, while similar to the first two bars, is not an exact transposition of measure 1; the left hand, as in the orchestral version, is transposed down eleven semitones, but the right hand is transposed down nine semitones. Since the instrument playing the line in the orchestral version is a B♭ clarinet, its notated part would read a whole tone higher than concert pitch. It seems likely, then, that the orchestral version came first, and that when Hanson (or perhaps an amanuensis) later transcribed that measure, he inadvertently transcribed the clarinet line from the score as written, rather than as sounded. There are other possible explanations, of course—perhaps Hanson changed only that single line between the two versions; or perhaps the solo piano version came first, and when Hanson conducted the recorded orchestral version he did not notice the solo clarinet playing an entire measure a whole tone too low, either during the recording or while listening to the recorded playback—but they seem far less likely. (Since the two versions are virtually identical except for this single measure, for convenience the piano version will be the one referred to and quoted hereinafter.)

On the other hand, despite this apparent priority of the orchestral version, the piece apparently originated from a set of pieces for piano solo. In the Howard Hanson Papers at the Sibley Music Library is a manuscript titled *Seven Pieces for Children,* written on four twelve-staff folio sheets, inscribed "To Alberta"; there are also fragmentary sketches of the seven pieces with the name "Alberta Hartshorn" on top.[190] Marilyn Plain, who compiled the catalog for the Hanson manuscript collection, found in her researches that Alberta Hartshorn was the daughter of the music supervisor of the Los Angeles school system, which sponsored school concerts featuring Hanson leading the Los Angeles Philharmonic during the late 1950s and early 1960s.

The relationship between this work and *For the First Time* is interesting. Each page of *Seven Pieces for Children* begins with a text written for a child. The first page begins as follows.

If you count seven half-steps
on the keyboard, like this:

you produce what is called the
<u>interval</u> <u>of</u> <u>the</u> <u>perfect</u> <u>fifth,</u>
(from C to G):

"The following two pieces are built on this interval." Then comes the first piece, "The Big Bell and the Little Bells," of which the first six measures are almost identical to the first three measures of *For the First Time*'s first movement, "Bells." (See Examples 6.2A and 6.2B for an illustration.) In the second piece, "More Bells," all but the first four measures correspond closely to the remainder of the published "Bells."

Example 6.2A   Hanson, *Seven Pieces for Children*, I, mm. 1–4

Example 6.2B   Hanson, *For the First Time*, I, mm. 1–2

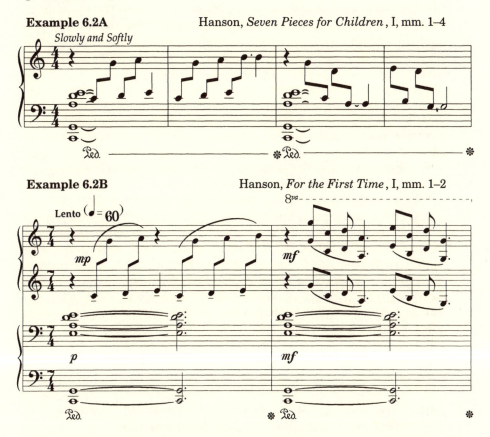

The third piece, "Mist," based on the interval of the major second, corresponds closely to the "Mist" movement in *For the First Time*, and there is a similar relation between the fourth piece, "Fireworks"—based on the minor third—and the "Fireworks" movement of *For the First Time*, and between the fifth piece, "Elves"—based on the major third—and the "Clowns" movement of *For the First Time*. On the other hand, the sixth piece, "Tricks or Treats," based on the minor second, bears little resemblance to "Tamara and Peter Bolshoi," the movement of *For the First Time*

based on the minor-second projection, except that like the latter it starts with the pitch classes C-D♭-C and has a similar texture and similar rhythmic gestures. See Examples 6.3A and 6.3B.

Example 6.3A   Hanson, *Seven Pieces for Children*, VI, mm. 1–3

Example 6.3B   Hanson, *For the First Time*, II, mm. 1–3

Similarly, the seventh piece, "Horn-Calls in the Forest," based on the augmented fourth, has no relation at all to "The Deserted House," the movement of *For the First Time* based on the "tritone projection," or to any of the other movements in the suite.

"The Big Bell and the Little Bells," "Tricks or Treats," and "Horn-Calls in the Forest" were published in 1964, the year after the orchestral version of *For the First Time* appeared, as part of *The New Scribner Music Library*, a collection for piano students of which Hanson served as Editor-in-Chief.[191] Although any reconstruction of the sequence of composition can only be speculative, it seems likely that Hanson, who had spent so many years dealing with these theoretical issues, first wrote these children's pieces for Alberta Hartshorn—perhaps with *The New Scribner Music Library* in mind, or perhaps even before the publication of *Harmonic Materials*—and then, in order to fulfil a commission from the Music Teachers National Association, decided to expand the idea to a full-fledged orchestral piece. Finally, at some point afterwards, he transcribed the suite for piano solo, thus returning the material to the genre in which it had begun.

In his notes and recorded analysis Hanson specifies a sonority for each movement, with each sonority projected up or down from C. In addition, almost every movement either begins or ends (or both) with the pitch class C. This helps to give a consistent C-centricity to a piece that otherwise, by its very nature, would have no tonal center. As befits a work with didactic intentions, virtually every movement begins with a prolonged presentation of the sonority, although no movement remains solely within the original harmony. Each one modulates in an accelerating harmonic rhythm, either to the original sonority in transposition or inversion, or to other sonorities that preserve a portion of the original. At the end, the original sonority usually returns. For example, "Mist" is based on the major-second hexad (or whole-tone scale). Of its thirty-one measures, the first eleven are entirely comprised of elements from the whole-tone scale C-D-E-F♯-G♯-A♯, measures 12 through 15 from the other whole-tone scale (D♭-E♭-F-G-A-C♭), measure 17 from the original scale, and measure 18 from the other scale. The next two climactic measures feature eighth-note augmented triads that alternate between the two whole-tone scales. (See Example 6.4.) The remainder of the movement is entirely based on the original whole-tone scale.

Example 6.4   Hanson, *For the First Time*, X, mm. 17–18

A more complex example is provided by "Dreams," a reproduction of which appears as Appendix C. Hanson tells us that it is based on the sonority C-F-G-A-B♭, which in his taxonomy is the pentad *pns* @ *s* (or *pns*/*s*), i.e., the projection of the triad *pns* at the major second or the minor seventh, C-G-A plus B♭-F-G (equivalent to sc 5-23 [02357]). The interval analysis of this sonority is $p^3mn^2s^3d$, showing that the predominant intervals are fifths and major seconds, followed by minor thirds. As Appendix C shows, measures 7 through 12 repeat the first six measures a perfect fourth higher, and measures 13 through the beginning of 16 repeat the first four measures a major second lower. The melody in the last half of measure 16 (E♭-F-G) makes a smooth transition to the next section, which is based on the sonority E♭-F-G-A-B♭-C-D, or P^6 (i.e., a six-fold projection of the perfect fifth, or sc 7-35 [013568T], the diatonic collection). Although this sonority would seem unrelated to the projection of *pns,* it does include the entire original sonority as a subset, and like the original its predominant intervals are fifths and major seconds, followed by minor thirds (interval analysis $p^6m^3n^4s^5d^2t$). On the last beat of measure 24 Hanson makes another transition, this time by altering D to D♭, to begin a four-measure section based on the sonority A♭-B♭-D♭-E♭-F-G, or *PNS* (i.e., the projection of *pns* upon itself—in this case, D♭-A♭-B♭ plus A♭-E♭-F plus B♭-F-G, or sc 6-33 [023579]). This sonority also, of course, includes the original *pns/s* sonority (transposed down a major second), and shares its preponderance of fifths and major seconds, followed by minor thirds (interval analysis $p^4m^2n^3s^4dt$). Measure 29 makes a transition back to P^6 with the alteration of A♭ to A in the melody in an adroit sequence. (See Example 6.5.) At measure 35 this resolves to a G major triad, of which the G-D dyad proves to be the beginning of a return to the opening music and the original *pns/s* sonority, transposed up a perfect fifth (G-C-D-E-F). When the F drops out, the end resolves with relative finality to C major with an added ninth; in Hanson's terms this sonority is p^2s^2, meaning that the predominant intervals are still fifths and major seconds. Nevertheless, this is a violation of the underlying premises of the work. (While such "violations" are comparatively rare and slight in the pieces examined in this chapter, they indicate a compositional tendency of Hanson's that will be discussed fully in the following chapters.)

Example 6.5   Hanson, *For the First Time*, XII, mm. 27–29

Even in a piece as short, simple, and relatively athematic as this, Hanson has been able, within the bounds of his system, to establish the balance between unity and variety, and between doctrine and freedom, that can be found in all good music. Although *For the*

First Time is relatively unambitious and "light," most of the other movements show a similar degree of skill and craftsmanship.

Nine years later Hanson wrote another piece to demonstrate the use of his theory, a Suite for Solo Piano, Winds and Percussion that has been published as *Young Person's Guide to the Six-Tone Scale*. Although this was apparently the original title, the holograph of the full score is entitled *Young People's Guide to the Six-Tone Scale, or Thirty-Five Scales in Search of Composers,* and it was premiered and recorded by the Eastman Wind Ensemble on Mercury, the recording label with which Hanson was affiliated, under the title *Young Composer's Guide to the Six Tone Scale*. In the Howard Hanson Papers, in addition to a holograph of the full score and detailed composition sketches in pencil, there is also an earlier score for piano and chamber wind ensemble under the original title.[192]

In his notes on *Young Person's Guide* Hanson writes:

My purpose has been to write a composition embracing every possible category of the six-tone scale. . . . The variations number thirty-five because there are thirty-five different categories of six-tone scales. . . . I suppose that I might sum up by saying that [this piece] is a light-hearted approach to a serious subject.[193]

He goes on to group the movements by the predominant interval in each. Variations #1 through #4 feature the fifth, #5 through #10 the major second, #11 through #15 the minor third, #16 through #21 the major third, #22 through #25 the minor second, #26 through #32 "the mysterious tritone," and #33 through #35 are "neutral, with no dominating interval." (The actual number of distinct hexachordal set classes is of course fifty, but the discrepancy is more apparent than real. The smaller figure of thirty-five comes from treating all "isomeric twins," or Z-related pairs, as equivalent. As we have seen, Hanson identifies fifty hexads or six-tone scales in *Harmonic Materials*; but in *Young Person's Guide to the Six-Tone Scale,* presumably to keep the piece to a manageable length, he treats each isomeric pair or quartet as belonging to the same category. Sometimes he uses them interchangeably within a movement, just as he uses both the original sonority and its involution.)

It is a curious piece, by any standard. For one thing, although Hanson refers to the thirty-five movements as "variations," they are not based on any theme; rather he seems to mean that they are variations on a central concept, each based upon one of the thirty-five types of hexads. In addition, while the work begins and ends in C, many of the movements are not based on projections beginning

on C, unlike *For the First Time.* The closest thing to a common
theme is the motivic cell with which the piece begins, a rising arpeg-
gio on C-G-B (in Hanson's terms, *pmd*), which recurs literally (in
#18), transposed (in #9), as a chord (in #20), and perhaps also more
freely, as a gesture of three notes rising through a seventh or a similar interval—as in #2, #3, #4, #5, #12, inverted in #13 and #28, in
#32 and at the end of #33 (normal and inverted), and briefly at the
end of #35 (inverted). The cell may also be present, transformed, at
the beginnings of #17, #29, and #30. (Example 6.6A shows three
possible versions of this cell.) As indicated in Example 6.6B, movements #2, #5, #11, #24, and #33 also share gestural similarities (a
reiterated fluttering on a downward major second—although #24
uses a minor second, and the pattern of #33 is considerably different); so do #20, #21, and #27 (a slow progression from one chord to
another by step motion—although in #20 the top line is a rising minor second and in the other two it is falling), as well as #29 and #30
(a rising three-note arpeggiated figure followed by a falling one,
perhaps related to the opening motive). Finally, a brief syncopated
waltz-like line in #22 seems to be alluded to in #28, although in the
latter the opening gesture outlines a tritone rather than a perfect
fourth, and the continuation of the line is different (Example 6.6C).

Example 6.6A   Hanson, *Young Person's Guide,* motivic transformations

Example 6.6B   Hanson, *Young Person's Guide,* motivic transformations

Example 6.6C   Hanson, *Young Person's Guide,* motivic transformations

Although the stated purpose of *Young Person's Guide* was to illustrate the thirty-five different types of hexads (treating isomeric
twins and quartets as equivalent), an analysis of its actual contents

reveals several puzzles. Table 6.2 shows the sonority or sonorities serving as the source material for each movement, each designated first by Hanson's symbols as used in Chapter 50 and the foldout master diagram in *Harmonic Materials*, then by its set-class designation. (Alternative terms used by Hanson follow his primary ones in parentheses. As with Table 6.1, numerical superscripts refer to projections, not to interval analysis. The term "inv." means that Hanson has used, or at least begun the movement with, the involution of the sonority as it is presented in *Harmonic Materials*.)

Hanson does not explain why the movements featuring perfect-fifth hexads are followed by those featuring major-second hexads, rather than by minor-second hexads—as would be the case if he followed the order used in the book—or by major-third hexads—as would be the case if he arranged the hexads in his purported order of increasing dissonance. Still, examination of Table 6.2 shows that, as one might expect, the order of movements within each grouping generally follows the order of presentation of the hexads used in *Harmonic Materials*. But Table 6.2 reveals another fact that is rather surprising. While Hanson has clearly implied that each of the thirty-five movements is based on one of the thirty-five types of hexads, this is not the case: two of the hexads, n^2/s (sc 6-Z23 [023568]) and $\updownarrow p^2 n^2 m^1$ (sc 6-Z46 [012469]), do not have their own movements. In the first place, the sonority of movement #14 is the isomeric twin (Z-correspondent) of the sonority that begins and ends #13, and thus, by Hanson's rules, is of the same type. (Hanson seems to provide a clue to this connection by beginning #14 with piano glissandi over silently depressed keys holding the pitches of the #13 sonority transposed up seven semitones.) Secondly, as can be seen from their set-class names, the two primary sonorities of movement #35 are not six-tone but five-tone sonorities.

Where, then, are the missing two hexads? Hanson has concealed them within movements dominated by other sonorities. The key to the puzzle is movement #13, chosen perhaps because of the folk superstitions commonly associated with the number. While this movement, a quiet and mysterious *Andantino*, begins with n^3+m^3 (as C-E♭-E-F♯-A♭-A, or sc 6-Z28 [013569]), the fourth measure "modulates," using four of the original tones as a pivot chord, to one of the missing hexads, n^2/s (sc 6-Z23 [023568]), followed by its isomeric twin n^3+s^3 (sc 6-Z45 [023469]). (See Example 6.7. All transcriptions hereinafter are by the author.) The fifth measure continues the alternation of n^2/s and n^3+s^3, the two following measures alternate five-tone subsets of each, and the ninth and tenth measures return to the n^3+s^3 sonority. In measure 11 the line continues with what appears to be a sequential transposition of n^3+s^3 five semi-

	Hanson term	equivalent set class
1.	P^5	6-32 [024579]
2.	$PNS\ (p^3s^3)$	6-33 [023579]
3.	$\updownarrow p^2s^2d^1$	6-Z47 [012479]
4.	p^2/m	6-Z26 [013578]
5.	S^6 *	6-35 [02468T]
6.	s^4p^2	6-22 [012468]
7.	$\uparrow s^4n^2\downarrow$	6-34 [013579]
8.	s^4n^2	6-21 [023468]
9.	pmd/s	6-9 [012357]
10.	s^2/n	6-8 [023457]
11.	N^5 inv.	6-27 [013469]
12.	$n^3{}_+p^3$	6-Z29 [023679]
13.	$n^3{}_+m^3$ (n^2/s)	6-Z28 [013569] (6-Z23 [023568])
14.	n^2/m	6-Z49 [013479]
15.	$n^3{}_+d^3$	6-Z42 [012369]
16.	M^6 *	6-20 [014589]
17.	PMN inv.	6-31 [014579]
18.	PMD	6-16 [014568]
19.	MND	6-15 [012458]

Table 6.2 (*continued*)

Hanson term	equivalent set class
20. pmd/n	6-14 [013458]
21. $\updownarrow p^2 m^2 d^1$	6-Z19 [013478]
22. D^5	6-1 [012345]
23. $NSD\ (s^3 d^3)$	6-2 [012346]
24. $\updownarrow n^2 s^2 d^1\ (pns/d)$	6-Z3 [012356]
25. d^2/m	6-Z4 [012456]
26. $T^3\ (p^2/t)*$	6-7 [012678]
27. pmn/t	6-30 [013679]
28. mst/p inv.	6-18 [012578]
29. mst/d	6-5 [012367]
30. p^2/d	6-Z38 [012378]
31. $\updownarrow p^2 d^2 s^1\ (pdt/s)$	6-Z41 [012368]
32. $\updownarrow p^2 d^2 m^1$ inv.	6-Z43 [012568]
33. $\updownarrow n^2 d^2 m^1\ (nsd/m)$	6-Z10 [013457]
34. $p^2 s^2 d^2{+}d\downarrow$ inv.	6-Z40 [012358]
35. $p^2 m^2\updownarrow, \uparrow s^2 n^2\downarrow$ $(\updownarrow p^2 n^2 m^1)$	5-Z17, 5-34 (6-Z46 [012469])

*Hanson's names for the sonorities used in movements #5, #16, and #26 are actually misnomers. As with the "T^3" and "S^6" sonorities (see Table 6.1), the correct name for the "M^6" sonority should be M^5, since it is the sonority produced by a fivefold major-third projection (although of necessity it includes a "foreign tone").

tones higher, although in fact it is only part of such a transposition, because it is a five-tone sonority, missing the D♮ necessary to make it n^3+s^3. (See Example 6.8.) This is followed by a measure which seems to be in the same sonority, but by adding an additional but "wrong" tone (the E♮), Hanson creates not n^3+s^3 but the involution of $\updownarrow p^2n^2m^1$ (sc 6-Z46 [012469]), the other missing sonority! The last two measures return to the opening sonority (without the F♯)—but now with a certain implied ambiguity, since all the tones of the first or "A♭" half of measure 2 can be found in n^2/s as well as in n^3+m^3, and all those of the second or "A minor" half can also be found in n^3+s^3.

Example 6.7   Hanson, *Young Person's Guide,* #13, mm. 1–4

Example 6.8   Hanson, *Young Person's Guide,* #13, mm. 9–12

There is also the puzzle of the two five-tone sonorities that dominate movement #35, the finale. (See a transcription of this movement in Appendix E.) The opening sonority $p^2m^2\updownarrow$ (C-E-F-G-A♭, or sc 5-Z17 [01348]) is the basis of measures 1 through 10 and 26 through 31, and the other pentad $\uparrow s^2n^2\downarrow$ (C-E♭-G♭-A♭-B♭, or sc 5-34 [02469]) is the basis of measures 13 and 14, and (transposed up a fifth) of measures 21 through 25, while its seven-tone complement (C-D-E-F♯-G-A-B♭) is the basis of measure 18. (Measures 19 and 20 make a transition between a G minor triad in the first three beats of measure 19, which is a "suspended" subset of the seven-tone complement of $\uparrow s^2n^2\downarrow$ from measure 18, and a B♭ minor triad in the last two beats of 19 and all of 20, which is an "anticipatory" subset of the $\uparrow s^2n^2\downarrow$ that reappears in measure 21.) So two apparently unrelated pentads form the basis of twenty-four out of the thirty-one measures of this movement.

Hanson, however, has one more trick up his sleeve, for which the "lucky" movement #13 again provides the clue. At the beginning of measure 11 of #35 there is a "modulation," and the "mystery" hexad $\updownarrow p^2 n^2 m^1$ (sc 6-Z46 [012469])—which has so far only appeared, in involution, for a single measure in movement #13—reappears for two measures, and two measures later its isomeric twin $p^2 m^2 s^1 \updownarrow$ (sc 6-Z24 [013468]) appears for three measures. Thus, if only for seven out of thirty-one measures, this movement does have a hexad as its basis. This may also solve the puzzle of the two pentads, because $p^2 m^2 \updownarrow$ (sc 5-Z17 [01348]) turns out to be a subset of $p^2 m^2 s^1 \updownarrow$, and $\uparrow s^2 n^2 \downarrow$ (sc 5-34 [02469]) to be a subset of $\updownarrow p^2 n^2 m^1$. This procedure of letting a subset temporarily "stand in" for a hexad is also used in the first two measures of movement #33, which begins with an alternation of the pentad $s^3 p^2$ (C-D-E-F♯-G, sc 5-24 [01357]) and the tetrad $p^2 s^2$ (C-E♭-A♭-B♭, sc 4-22 [0247]). Both of these are subsets of the hexad $\updownarrow n^2 d^2 m^1$ (sc 6-Z10 [013457]), which does not enter until the third measure—although after that, it dominates the entire movement. Movement #35, however, is structured like a puzzle box with a surprise hidden inside.

Hanson gives no explanation for these strange displacements, but based on his well-known sense of humor, one might hazard a guess. Since in his own words he wrote the piece "as a kind of joke... more like a crossword puzzle sort of thing, I had a lot of fun doing it,"[194] and since he begins movement #22 with a quote from the popular piano tune "Chopsticks," it seems likely that he deliberately concealed the two sonorities, and yet left clues connecting their locations, as a private joke on future analysts who might be looking for the expected correspondences.

Although the longest movement lasts about one minute and fifteen seconds, and the shortest only twenty seconds, and despite the severe limitations of the task Hanson has set himself, *Young Person's Guide* shows considerable skill in weaving interesting and varied music out of limited material, to a greater extent than *For the First Time*—which, of course, he always considered to some extent a children's piece. Virtually every movement has a unique sound world, due not only to the nature of the piece but also to Hanson's lively and inventive instrumentation. Movement #34, although extremely short, provides an illustration of his thoroughness in utilizing his given harmonic resources and in deriving maximum tonal variety from them, as well as his skill at dovetailing and eliding his transitions to make them seamless. (See Appendix D. Since this entire movement is for piano solo, except for a bassoon part that doubles inner lines of the piano part, only the piano part is reproduced.)

Measure 1 contains a statement of the basic $p^2s^2d^2+d\downarrow$ sonority (B♭-C♭-E♭-G♭-A♭-A, sc 6-Z40 [012358]), although this statement is not completed until the melody lands on G♭ on the downbeat of measure 2. (To avoid confusion in the following discussion, this sonority will be labelled $p^2s^2d^2+d\downarrow$ or "the original," but anyone looking for it in *Harmonic Materials* should be reminded that, as shown in Table 6.2, Hanson lists it as the *involution* of $p^2s^2d^2+d\downarrow$.)[195] This G♭ is also the beginning of a measure based on the involution of the sonority (B-C-D♭-E♭-G♭-B♭), which is itself not completely stated until the melody note B♭ on the downbeat of measure 3. The next two measures return to the original sonority. The sonority of measures 5 and 6, $p^2s^2d^2+p\downarrow$ (B-C♯-D-E-E♯-F♯, sc 6-Z11 [012457]), is the isomeric twin of the original sonority. Measure 7 is based on the involution of this twin sonority (D-E♭-E-F♯-G-A), while measure 8 is based on the involution of the original sonority, transposed up a semitone (C-D♭-D-E-G-B). As at the beginning, this sonority is not fully heard until the melody note B on the downbeat of measure 9. This ushers in what might be termed a "recapitulation," a return to the beginning material transposed up a semitone, with slight differences in register and doubling. Measures 11 and 12, which could be said to constitute a "codetta," actually repeat the material of measure 7, transposed up a major second (E-F-F♯-G♯-A-B). Hanson retains only the E, G♯ and B in the last measure to close with an E major triad. In a harmonic sense, Hanson achieves maximum variety in this movement by the use of all four basic forms of the sonority in various transpositions, and by the selective choice and deployment of tones from each form. The motivic saturation created by the use of the initial descending motif throughout the movement, and the overlapping of the different forms through pivot tones, bind together what might have been perceived as disparate harmonies into a unified whole with a beginning, middle and end.

Further evaluation of the two "demonstration pieces" will be reserved for the end of the next chapter, but for now we can summarize the above discussion by concluding that in both *For the First Time* and *Young Person's Guide to the Six-Tone Scale* Hanson succeeded in at least his two self-imposed tasks: both are entertaining, and both demonstrate that with Hanson's system as a guide or resource, a composer can write music that is technically accomplished and accessible.

Chapter 7

The Influence of the Theory on Hanson's Later Compositions

We are now ready to consider the question of the extent and nature of the influence exerted by Hanson's theory on his compositions other than the two "demonstration pieces" discussed in the previous chapter. As previously mentioned, late in life Hanson said, "I think all of the later works were influenced [by the theory]. I mean, you can't be working as intensively as I was for forty years on that theory without being automatically influenced. And I was always fascinated by how much logic there is in musical progression."[196] In other remarks in the same interview, however, he made clear that he did not believe that all his later pieces were perceptibly influenced by the system, nor that all the pieces that had been influenced were influenced to the same degree. For our purposes three representative works will be examined in detail, and three others more briefly, all of which were written after a time by which Hanson's theory had been essentially formulated. This *terminus a quo* is taken to be approximately the year 1951, because at that point Hanson had been teaching the theory for several years, had made its essentials public, and was (or believed himself to be) about to publish it, although the actual publication took another nine years.

The pieces to be examined in this chapter—*Sinfonia Sacra* (1955), *Elegy* (1956), Symphony no. 6 (1968), and more briefly *Mosaics* (1958), *A Sea Symphony* (1977), and *Nymph and Satyr* (1979)— have been chosen to illustrate a range of different degrees of the theory's influence. Hanson felt that *Mosaics* and Symphony no. 6 show a strong influence, and that *Sinfonia Sacra* and *A Sea Symphony* show little or no influence. He mentioned *Nymph and Satyr* as showing some influence, at least at the precompositional stage.[197] He did not mention the *Elegy* as either influenced or not; the reasons for its inclusion here will become evident when it is examined, later in this chapter.

Nor did Hanson specify the ways in which he believed the theory had exerted influence on his music. However, we can derive our own criteria for gauging the extent of influence: from his comments on the use of the theory in composition (in *Harmonic Materials*), from our analyses of the two "demonstration pieces" (in the previous chapter) and Hanson's own comments on the theory's role in their composition (in his liner notes and oral commentaries), and to a lesser extent from his analyses of other composers' music. We will gauge the extent of influence from the extent to which a work displays the following criteria: restriction of harmonic or melodic vocabulary to a limited number of sonorities or projections; a demonstrable interrelatedness among the predominant sonorities; the use of triadic formations primarily as subsets of larger nontriadic sonorities, rather than in their traditional harmonic roles; and harmonic motion based primarily on processes of expansion or contraction of sonorities, rather than on functional harmony.[198]

We will begin with *Sinfonia Sacra* (Symphony no. 5), a piece in one movement which, according to Hanson, attempts "to invoke the atmosphere of tragedy and triumph" of the story of the resurrection in the Gospel of St. John.[199] This stark, brooding work has a massive power, with a certain emotional reserve characteristic of many of Hanson's middle-period works. The primary thematic material is shown in Examples 7.1A through 7.1F.

Example 7.1A   Hanson, *Sinfonia Sacra*, mm. 1–3

Example 7.1B   Hanson, *Sinfonia Sacra*, m. 3 after rehearsal 4

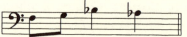

Example 7.1C   Hanson, *Sinfonia Sacra,* mm. 1–2 after rehearsal 6

Example 7.1D   Hanson, *Sinfonia Sacra,* mm. 11–13 after rehearsal 7

Example 7.1E   Hanson, *Sinfonia Sacra,* mm. 1–2 after rehearsal 9

Example 7.1F   Hanson, *Sinfonia Sacra,* m. 1 before – m. 4 after rehearsal 12

While this piece cannot be said to be in any traditional form, it is essentially tripartite. In the first part, a slow introduction that develops motif *x* (Example 7.1A) and includes subsidiary motifs such as 7.1B leads to a strong, agonized tutti theme (Example 7.1C) which, after further elaboration of *x* and a series of falling thirds that introduce a theme in the bass (7.1D), leads to a section based on a theme (7.1E) reminiscent of Lutheran chorales. (As mentioned in Chapter 2, and as he himself acknowledged, the use of chorale-like themes is a stylistic fingerprint of Hanson's. He attributed it to the influence of the Swedish Lutheran church that he had attended in childhood.)[200] The short second part is dominated by a melancholy theme first played by the English horn (7.1F). This builds steadily through a tremendous stretto into the final part, which begins with a return of the big tutti theme (7.1C), followed by a brass canon, a return of the bass theme (7.1D), and a furious "development" (which is itself in a loose ternary form), with quickly alternating triads over pedal points, primarily utilizing x, 7.1B, and 7.1E as motivic material. This culminates in a climax of violent short tutti chords. The final section is a return to the "chorale" section that begins with the brass, builds to a second tutti climax, and then subsides to quiet bitonal chords.

Analysis of this work, to a considerable extent, supports Hanson's opinion that it is essentially uninfluenced by his theory. While a number of perceptibly nontriadic sonorities appear more than once, few appear often enough to be considered fundamental compositional elements. Rather, as the opening material (Example 7.1A) suggests, this function is served more by triads, major and minor, and by their various conjunctions. The opening two measures, which according to Hanson's theory would constitute sonority M^5 ($p^3m^6n^3d^3$, or sc 6-20 [014589], the hexatonic collection), can also be said to consist of a series of triads in first inversion, each of which begins with a minor third that resolves to a major one in a rising appoggiatura (C and E triads in measure 1, then C, E, and A♭ in measure 2). This sonority appears again three measures later, in a variant of the opening measures (transposed up a major third and compressed from two measures into one), and after that the M^5 sonority is not heard again, except for one or two isolated measures. The same is true for the *pdt* sonority (sc 3-5 [016]) of measure 3.

What can be found over and over, however, is the conjunction of two (or more) major or minor triads (or occasionally dominant sevenths), either as bitonal simultaneities, or in close alternation, or both. As mentioned in Chapter 2, the use of parallel or alternating triads is another stylistic fingerprint of Hanson's, though to a lesser extent than in the works of Debussy or Vaughan Williams. It can be found in most of his works from Symphony no. 1 (1922) through *Nymph and Satyr* (1979), and is especially prevalent in *Sinfonia Sacra*. In addition to Example 7.1D, several more such conjunctions are shown in Examples 7.2A through 7.2E.

While all of these juxtapositions involve major or minor triads (which in the theory are equivalent), the sonorities produced by each are quite different. Example 7.2A forms the $m^2n^2\ddagger$ sonority (sc 5-22 [01478]); 7.2B forms *pmn/s* or *PNS* (sc 6-33 [023579]); 7.2C forms $n^3 + p^3$ (sc 6-Z29 [023679]); 7.2D, the climactic chords, form *pmn/t* (sc 6-30

Example 7.2A Hanson, *Sinfonia Sacra*, m. 2 before rehearsal 2

Example 7.2B Hanson, *Sinfonia Sacra,* mm. 7–9 after rehearsal 3

Example 7.2C Hanson, *Sinfonia Sacra,* mm. 1–2 before rehearsal 32

Example 7.2D Hanson, *Sinfonia Sacra,* mm. 1–2 after rehearsal 34

Example 7.2E Hanson, *Sinfonia Sacra,* mm. 1–2 after rehearsal 39

[013679], the "Petrushka chord"); and 7.2E, the begining of the quiet coda, again forms $n^3 + p^3$. Even parallel and apparently identical places in the score do not necessarily correspond in terms of interval content. Example 7.3B, which follows Example 7.3A by three measures, resembles it so strongly as to appear to be a simple transposition, or a change of pedal point; but while the sonority in Example 7.3A would be C. $n^2p^1\updownarrow$ (sc 8-27 [0124578T]), Example 7.3B would be C. $pmnsdt$ (sc 8-Z15 [01234689]). What they do have in common harmonically is the alternation of three major triads over a sustained pedal point: in the first, A, C♯, and G triads over B; in the second, C, F♯, and G triads over D.

Example 7.3A   Hanson, *Sinfonia Sacra*, mm. 2–3 after rehearsal 27

Example 7.3B   Hanson, *Sinfonia Sacra,* mm. 6–7 after rehearsal 27

Examples 7.4A and 7.4B are similar: While the sonority in 7.4B is motivically parallel to, and sounds like a transposed version of, the one in 7.4A, the latter would be pmn/t (sc 6-30 [013679]) and the former pmn/d or $\updownarrow p^7m^7d^1$ (sc 6-Z44 [012569]). Harmonically they have in common only the alternation of two major triads over a pedal: in the first E and B♭ over D, in the second A and B♭ over F. (Example 7.4 only reproduces the pitches played by the brass and timpani; other tones have been omitted for this illustration.)

Example 7.4A   Hanson, *Sinfonia Sacra*, m. 1 after rehearsal 32

Example 7.4B   Hanson, *Sinfonia Sacra*, m. 5 after rehearsal 32

Nevertheless, there are three sonorities that are not triads and yet are too prevalent to be considered incidental to this piece. The first, in Hanson's terminology called C. N^3 (sc 8-28 [0134679T], usually known as the octatonic collection), is the aggregate of all tones between rehearsal 20 and 22, and (transposed up a semitone) between rehearsal 25 and 26. The second is the sonority that Hanson would call C. $\uparrow s^2 n^2 \downarrow$ (sc 7-34 [013468T]) but is more commonly known as the ascending melodic minor scale; it appears for five measures beginning at rehearsal 5, for three measures beginning at three after 7, for the four measures before 11, for two measures beginning at four after 15, for two isolated measures between 35 and 36, and for two measures beginning at 37. The third is the sonority that Hanson calls P^6 (sc 7-35 [013568T]) but is usually known as the diatonic collection, the major scale, or the natural minor scale; it appears for most of the first "chorale" section, between rehearsal 8 and five measures before 11 (sounding as E minor or E major), for almost all of the middle interlude between rehearsal 12 and 18 (as E minor, E Dorian, A Dorian, or A minor), and for almost all of the reprise of the "chorale" section between 35 and 39 (as E minor or A minor). Nevertheless, while these sonorities are not triads, there is little evidence that Hanson was thinking of them in terms of his theory. There is nothing in the first "octatonic" section to show any special importance given to minor thirds (*n*) in melody, harmony, or bass line; and the smooth alternation between the other two sonorities in both the interlude (Example 7.5A) and the "chorale" reprise (Example 7.5B) suggests strongly that Hanson thought of these essentially as different modal inflections of one tonality (E in both examples) rather than as two unrelated sonorities.

Example 7.5A   Hanson, *Sinfonia Sacra*, mm. 3–4 after rehearsal 15

Example 7.5B   Hanson, *Sinfonia Sacra*, mm. 1–2 after rehearsal 35

On the other hand, the second octatonic section (between rehearsal 25 and 26), based on the material in Example 7.1D, is saturated with minor thirds, both in the bass theme (the contours and strong beats of which all indicate minor thirds) and in the accompaniment; this section indeed seems to be constructed on a minor-third projection. We will reserve a final discussion of the theory's influence on *Sinfonia Sacra* for the end of this chapter.

We may also briefly consider Hanson's choral Symphony no. 7, *A Sea Symphony*—another work that "isn't at all" influenced by the theory, as he asserted shortly after he had finished it.[201] While much of this piece is based on diatonic or modal sonorities, the beginning is as clear an example of the four-tone perfect-fifth projection as he ever wrote (Example 7.6).

Example 7.6   Hanson, *A Sea Symphony*, I, mm. 1–2

Also in this movement is a passage in which one measure (Example 7.7A) based on what might be called an F major chord over a G pedal, but could also be said to be based on the C-F-G-A or p^2s^2 tetrad (sc 4-22 [0247]), is followed—after three intervening measures based on the opening of the Symphony no. 2, which is deliberately quoted several times in this piece—by several measures based on the eight-tone complement of the tetrad (C♯-D-D♯-E-F♯-G♯-A♯-B, sc 8-22 [0123568T]; see Example 7.7B), followed by several measures based on a seven-tone subset of the eight-tone complement, produced by omitting the D♯ (C♯-D-E-F♯-G♯-A♯-B, sc 7-34 [013468T]; see Example 7.7C).[202]

Example 7.7A   Hanson, *A Sea Symphony*, I, rehearsal 3

Example 7.7B   Hanson, *A Sea Symphony*, I, m. 5 after rehearsal 3

Example 7.7C   Hanson, *A Sea Symphony*, I, rehearsal 4

Thus we see another example of a piece on which, as far as Hanson was concerned, the theory had no influence, and which nevertheless shows some evidence of structures and procedures that are straight out of *Harmonic Materials*.

Let us now consider a Hanson piece about which, in terms of the theory's influence, he made no comment. The *Elegy* is a short work for orchestra, written in memory of the conductor Serge Koussevitsky. It is in an extremely loose ternary form, but gives the impression of continuous development, transformation, and combination of a few basic motives until the very end. The pace is slow and the mood is appropriately sad and restrained, although the music rises to several climaxes during the course of the piece, and the overall effect is of haunting and melancholy beauty. The primary compositional material is given in Examples 7.8A through 7.8D. Example 7.8A is the opening and most important theme; 7.8B is a subsidiary theme that first occurs about a minute into the piece, and later provides the last climax; the alternating chords of 7.8C occur at the other climactic moments; and 7.8D is a subsidiary theme (based on a neighbor-tone figure deriving from the second measure of the opening theme) that occurs twice in the middle section of the piece. In addition there are two brief quotations from pieces Hanson had written for Koussevitsky: The two measures before rehearsal number 3 contain a slightly altered quotation from the lyrical second theme of his Symphony no. 2, and the last two measures quote the opening motto theme of his Concerto for Piano and Orchestra.

Example 7.8A   Hanson, *Elegy*, mm. 1–2

Example 7.8B   Hanson, *Elegy*, mm. 1–2 after rehearsal 6

Example 7.8C   Hanson, *Elegy*, m. 4 before rehearsal 9

Example 7.8D   Hanson, *Elegy*, mm. 1–6 after rehearsal 9

Although this piece makes little use of traditional functional harmony, there is considerable use of diatonicism, triads, and triadic structures. Indeed, in several places a major triad is sustained—at rehearsal number 5 for six measures, at rehearsal 7 for four measures, and at rehearsal 20 for four measures—and the piece ends conclusively on an E major triad.

Nevertheless, there are many sonorities in *Elegy* that cannot be analyzed as traditional tonal structures. The opening theme (Example 7.8A), with its elaboration, gives the sense of an alternation between a harmony centered on C (or C minor), and one centered on E (or E minor); but Hanson saw both measures as part of a single sonority, C-D-E♭-E-G-B, or *pmd/n* ($p^3m^4n^3s^2d^3$, sc 6-14 [013458]). This can be asserted not only because Hanson characteristically thought of alternating harmonies as halves of a single sonority (as discussed in the fifth chapter of this book), but because at the beginning of a sketch for *Elegy*, he listed the tones of the theme and the interval succession, and added the notation *pmd/n*.[203] This sonority recurs literally only at the end of the piece, but with various tones added it also appears slightly past the halfway point (from rehearsal 12 to two measures before 14), where it serves to begin the final section of the piece.

In addition, at the place in the sketch corresponding to the eighth measure after rehearsal number 13 in the score (Example 7.9) can be found the listing of the tones E-G-A-B-C-D♯, the interval succession 3-2-2-1-3-1, and the notation n^3p^3. This sonority is known as *PMN*, or $p^3m^4n^3s^2d^2t$ (sc 6-31 [014579]), in Hanson's last chapter and on his master diagram. The n^3p^3 notation is either an error or uses a earlier symbology than that in the published version of *Harmonic*

Materials; if its meaning were $n^3 + p^3$, i.e., the projection of three minor thirds and three fifths above a given note, the interval succession would be 2-3-2-1-3-1, and the sequence of tones (starting on E as in the score) would be E-F♯-A-B-C-D♯. Nevertheless, the fact remains that Hanson was thinking of specific sonorities from his system, at least in certain parts of the piece.

Example 7.9   Hanson, *Elegy*, m. 121

One of the compositional techniques that Hanson seems to have developed from his theory is a process of gradual expansion from a smaller sonority to a larger one. This is illustrated by the beginning of the piece (Example 7.10).[204]

Example 7.10   Hanson, *Elegy*, mm. 1–10

The initial motif, as already stated, derives from the sonority *pmd/n* (sc 6-14 [013458]). The addition of A in measure 4 creates the sonority C. *pmn/p* ($p^5m^4n^4s^4d^3t$, sc 7-27 [0124579]), which persists for three more measures; measures 7–8 add A♭ and F♯ to create C. *pmn* ($p^7m^7n^7s^6d^6t^3$, sc 9-11 [01235679T]); and measures 9–10 subtract A♭ and add C♯ and F to create C. *s* (sc 10-2 [012345678T]). This lasts until the third beat of measure 13, where the transition to the second section of the piece begins. The original six-tone *pmd/n* "core" remains as these changes produce increasingly more complex sonorities. A similar process occurs, as mentioned above, at the beginning of the final section, when the opening theme returns.

Hanson uses a somewhat different procedure in the transition from the opening to the Symphony no. 2 quotation. See Example 7.11.

Example 7.11   Hanson, *Elegy*, mm. 14–28

At the beginning of this excerpt the sonority (C-D-E♭-G-A♭-B♭) is p^2/m ($p^4m^3n^2s^3d^2t$, sc 6-Z26 [013578]). In measures 17–19, Hanson subtracts the E♭ and B♭ and adds F, making C-D-F-G-A♭, or ↑p^2n^2↓ ($p^3mn^2s^2dt$, sc 5-29 [01368]); in measures 20–23 he subtracts A♭, leaving P^3 (p^3ns^2, sc 4-23 [0257]); in measure 24 he adds back A♭ and B♭, making C-D-F-G-A♭-B♭ or *PNS* ($p^4m^2n^3s^4dt$, sc 6-33 [023579]); in measures 25–26 he adds E, making C. ↑s^2n^2↓ ($p^4m^4n^4s^5d^2t^2$, sc 7-34

[013468T]). Finally in measures 27–28 Hanson subtracts three tones, leaving C-D-E-G, or p^2s^2 (p^3mns^2, sc 4-22 [0247]), from which he then goes on to the Symphony no. 2 quotation by transposing the sonority up a semitone and adding two more tones. The entire passage can be said to show a "modulation" made by gradually expanding and contracting a sonority.

Also worth noting briefly is an extended sequence based on the motif shown in Example 7.8B. (See Example 7.12.) The sequence begins at rehearsal 16 in the C. p^2m^2 sonority (sc 7-30 [0124689]), then after three measures, by altering the D♯ to a D♮, "modulates" to P^6 (sc 7-35 [013568T], the diatonic collection). This sonority predominates until rehearsal 20; as the statements of the motif steadily ascend sequentially, going up by one scale degree in every measure, the P^6 sonority moves by transposition, first up a major third after three measures (at rehearsal 17), then up a fourth after three measures, then up another fourth after four measures, and then down a semitone at the last climax (rehearsal 19) as the dynamics slowly diminish and the motif descends.

Example 7.12   Hanson, *Elegy*, mm. 3–4 after rehearsal 16

All of the above are examples of processes derived from Hanson's theory and his concept of projection. As with the other works under discussion, final consideration of the theory's influence on the *Elegy* will be reserved until the end of this chapter.

We may also briefly consider *Nymph and Satyr*, the last piece Hanson completed.[205] This tuneful, mellow work began as two separate concertante pieces, a Fantasy for solo clarinet and chamber orchestra, and a Scherzo for solo bassoon and chamber orchestra. Shortly after he completed these, Hanson added a Prelude and an Epilogue to make a "ballet suite" which was premiered by the Chautauqua Ballet. This piece is unusual in that Hanson has left some description of how he began to write it, or at least the clarinet Fantasy movement:

In this case, I've always been fascinated by the notes C-D-F, in whatever key, in the combination of the major second with the minor third above it—perfect fourth on the outer ends—and I just began working with that interval, and finally out of it came a tune. . . . This piece starts out with the violins playing C and D and then the F is added; then the clarinets start C-D-F, D-E-G, F-G-B♭, making parallel motions up.[206]

This is a clear description of a piece that begins with the *pns* sonority (sc 3-7 [025]), which is then projected onto itself to form the *PNS* hexad (sc 6-33 [023579]), and the Fantasy movement does indeed begin this way.

Example 7.13   Hanson, *Nymph and Satyr*, II, mm. 1–5

There are also several passages that show the kind of "modulation" of a sonority by expansion or contraction that we have seen in the *Elegy*. But this "by the book" opening could also be heard and interpreted as a simple diatonic opening, gradually revealing a dominant eleventh chord; and most of *Nymph and Satyr* is dominated by simple diatonic harmonies (usually major, minor, Lydian, or pentatonic) and even functional dominant-tonic cadences, with only the slightest and the most conventional of chromatic inflections.

Let us now turn, in contrast, to the Symphony no. 6, a work that Hanson explicitly said was strongly influenced by the theory. In its six alternating slow and fast movements this symphony, like the *Sinfonia Sacra* and the *Elegy*, shows considerably less melodic lyricism and lush harmony than many of Hanson's earlier works. Functional harmony is almost completely dispensed with in favor of more modern "pantonal" means of progression and development, although there is still some use of triadic structures on the small scale. There is a demonic drive and hammering, violent power in the fast movements that is unusual in Hanson's work, and the overall effect of the contrasting movements is somewhat enigmatic, like different views of a domineering, discordant personality that combine to create a multifaceted and somewhat contradictory portrait.

Ten years after the writing of this symphony, when a former student remarked that the symphony shows a strong influence of the theory, Hanson agreed, saying: "The Sixth [Symphony] . . . is built on one three-tone chord, the perfect fifth with a major second on top of it. C-G-A with all of its variations, permutations and extensions. That was, I think, to some degree conscious."[207] Hanson did not specify what he meant by "variations, permutations and extensions," but during the following discussion it should be borne in mind that the influence of the theory will be gauged in the same way it has already been gauged: in terms of the consistency of interval relations.

The symphony begins with the notes C-G-A. (See Appendix F for a transcription of the first movement.) In *Harmonic Materials* this sonority, like the one that opens the second movement of *Nymph and Satyr*, would be called *pns*, i.e., a perfect fifth, a major second, and a minor third (sc 3-7 [025]). From Hanson's above remarks, one would expect to find the symphony saturated with appearances of *pns* as well as its "higher-order projections" of four, five, six, seven, eight, and nine tones. (The projection of *pns* can be found in Chapter 42 of *Harmonic Materials* on pp. 288–89, reproduced in this book as Appendix H.)

It is unarguable that the opening C-G-A, as a thematic motif, is an important element of the first movement (and, to a smaller extent, of the remaining movements). A rising fifth followed by a rising major second can be found, not only in measure 1, but in measures 3, 4, and 5, toward the end of the movement in measures 34, 36, 38, 40, and also inverted in 41–42. In addition, *pns* can be found in the second half of the opening phrase (i.e., with the addition of the bass note, F-E♭-C), and in such places as the first three notes of the violin line in measure 6, and the first three notes of the woodwind line in measure 7.

Nevertheless, such motivic connections do not ensure a consistency of sonorities such as those found in *For the First Time* and *Young Person's Guide*. When the first movement is analyzed as the other works in this chapter have been analyzed—by analyzing an entire phrase or simultaneity, in the same way that Hanson analyzes all the excerpts in *Harmonic Materials*—it emerges that *pns* is by no means predominant in the first movement. For example, the first phrase forms the sonority C-E♭-F-G-A, which Hanson calls $\uparrow s^2 n^2 \downarrow$ (or $p^2 n^2 \updownarrow$) and analyzes as $p^2 m^2 n^2 s^3 t$ (or sc 5-34 [02469]; *Harmonic Materials*, p. 363). This is not a part of the *pns* "family tree," although Hanson would consider it related at one remove, in the sense that it is a subset of *PNS*, the "*pns* hexad" C-E♭-F-G-A-B♭ (sc 6-33 [023579]).[208] It is true that in measures 3–4 an oboe line (with an echo in the flute) consists of the tones C-D-E♭-E-F-G-A, in Hanson's terms the complement of the *pns/s* pentad (sc 7-23 [0234579]), which pentad is a member of the *pns* projection that Hanson analyzes as consisting of two *pns* triads a major second apart.[209] However, in measures 4–5 the overlapping echoes from the clarinet, bassoon, and horn, consisting of the tones C-D-E-F♯-G-A-B♭, form the complement of the original $\uparrow s^2 n^2 \downarrow$ sonority; and the sonority sustained for four beats in measures 5–6 consists of C-F♯-G-B♭, which form the tetrad *pmnsdt* (sc 4Z-15 [0146], one of the all-interval tetrachords), with no relation to the *pns* projection except that it does, of course, include *pns* as a subset. Then the line in the violins in measure 6 forms the hexad *PNS*, and the woodwind continuation in measure 7 forms *PNS*. In combination with the *pmnsdt* tetrad the violin line forms the octad C. P^3 or $p^7 m^4 n^5 s^6 d^4 t^2$ (sc 8-23 [0123578T]), which appears to have no special connection to *pns* in Hanson's theory. However, with some effort it can be found to be one of the five possible "connecting octads" between the *pns* heptads and the *pns* nonad, making it a member of the *pns* projection. (See Appendix H. In set theory, sc 8-23 maximizes sc 3-7 or *pns*—i.e., there are more occurrences of 3-7 in this set class than of any other three-tone sonority, and more occurrences than in any other eight-tone sonority. This can also be found in Hanson's system by comparing the occurrences of *p*, *n*, and *s* in the interval analyses of all octads.)

On the other hand, in measures 9–10 similar rising lines form the sonority C-D-E♭-F-F♯-G-A♭-B♭-B, forming the complement of *pmn* ($p^7 m^7 n^7 s^6 d^6 t^3$, sc 9-11 [01235679T]), which again has no connection to *pns*, nor does any identifiable line or simultaneity in the next twelve measures (between rehearsal numbers 1 and 2). Three measures after rehearsal 1 the Violin I part consists of two rising figures of which the first, G-A-C, is unquestionably *pns*, while the second, B♭-D-E, is *mst* (sc 3-8 [026]), and the other similar figures in the same section are neither. (The passage from three measures before rehearsal 2 to rehearsal 3 consists of four groups of four rising three-note figures, each group representing a different partitioning of the chromatic collection; each three-note figure is either a major, minor, diminished, or augmented triad.) The original theme returns as a coda in measure 34; it again consists of $\uparrow s^2 n^2 \downarrow$ (sc 5-34 [02469]) and, in conjunction with the clarinet and oboe lines in measures 35–36, forms the complement of $\uparrow s^2 n^2 \downarrow$ (C-D-E♭-F-G-A-B, sc 7-34 [013468T]), which is followed by a line on bassoon that consists of *PNS* (C-D-E♭-F-A♭-B♭), then by four-and-a-half measures in the woodwinds, which again form the complement of $\uparrow s^2 n^2 \downarrow$ (C-D-E-F♯-

G♯-A-B); but the last two measures consist of *pmn/n* (D♭-E♭-F♯-A-B♭, sc 5-32 [01469]), and the final simultaneity is F♯-A-D♭, or *pmn* (sc 3-11 [037]).

A similar lack of intervallic consistency is true of the entire symphony. For example, after an introduction on unpitched percussion, the opening of the second movement (like the opening of the first movement) features a rising motif that begins with *pns* and consists of the ↑*s²n²*↓ sonority (C-E♭-F-G-A), but this sonority does not persist. (See Example 7.14A.) Four measures later, an extension of the opening motif in the bass is answered in the treble by what sounds like the same line transposed up a fifth (Example 7.14B); but there are two alterations, so that the answer (on the upper staff) begins on *pmd* (sc 3-4 [015]), and the answer as a whole is constructed not from G-B♭-C-D-E, which would be a transposition of the opening motif, but from G-B-C-D-E♭ or *p²m²↕* (*p²m³n²sd²*, sc 5-Z17 [01348]), which is unrelated to the original sonority. This variant is heard again at rehearsal 8, and another variant, *pmn/p* (*p³m²n²s²d*, sc 5-27 [01358]), is heard at rehearsal 16 (Example 7.14C).

Example 7.14A   Hanson, Symphony no. 6, II, m. 1–2 after rehearsal 5

Example 7.14B   Hanson, Symphony no. 6, II, m. 5 after rehearsal 5

Example 7.14C   Hanson, Symphony no. 6, II, m. 3 after rehearsal 16

Various harmonies predominate throughout the movement: C. *pmn/n* (sc 7-32 [0134689]) beginning at rehearsal 6, *M³* (sc 4-19 [0148]) at 7, ↕*p²m²s* (sc 6-Z24 [013468]) at 9, *m²n²↕* (sc 5-26 [02458], of which *M³* is a subset) at 10, *n³ + p³* (sc 6-Z29 [023679]) at 11, *p²d↕* (sc 4-

16 [0157]) at six measures after 12, $n^2m^1\updownarrow$ (sc 4-18 [0147]) at 13, pmn/p (sc 5-27 [01358]) at 16, $m^2n^2\updownarrow$ again at three measures before 18, and so forth. None of these sonorities are closely related to pns or to its projection. (Most of these contain pns, but so do all except seven of the thirty-eight pentads.) In addition, this movement is full of alternating major and minor triads.

While there is no consistency of interval relations throughout this movement, Examples 7.14A through 7.14C indicate a more traditional connection unifying the movement and the symphony as a whole. The statements of the theme in Example 7.14B and Example 7.14C are chromatically altered variants of the original theme in Example 7.14A, and it seems clear that the alterations of the theme dictated the change in sonorities, rather than the other way around. Of course, such transformation of motivic material has been a common feature of tonal music for centuries, and it is hardly surprising that it should function as a basic structural device in music as rooted in tradition as Hanson's.

A similar process of motivic variation can be seen in the diverse intervallic content of the three-note rising figures in the first movement, and in the extension of the opening theme of the last movement. (See Example 7.15. Omitted from this reduction are a timpani C at the downbeat of measure 1 and and a horn doubling of the first four notes of measure 9.)

Example 7.15   Hanson, Symphony no. 6, VI, mm. 1–9 (theme)

While the basic motive, set forth in the first two measures and repeated in the next two, belongs to the pns sonority (sc 3-7 [025]), its extension does not; measures 6–8 consist of p^2s (sc 3-9 [027]), measure 9 (repeated in measure 10) is simply t, and the combined sonority is $\uparrow p^2n^2\downarrow$ (sc 5-29 [01368]). It seems clear that the formative impulse of this theme (and of similar passages later in the movement) is a gradual augmentation of the original rising interval, from a

minor third to a fourth and then to a tritone. This is a melodic procedure, unrelated to intervallic consistency.

Similarly, it should come as no surprise that there are intercon-
nections, allusions and quotations of themes and motives between
movements. Hanson's assertion that the entire symphony "is built
on one three-tone chord . . . with all of its variations, permutations
and extensions" may be considered generally true in the traditional
symphonic sense, but hardly in the sense of his theory. The primary
melodic material of the symphony is derived from any and all of the
following: "the Perfect fifth with a major second on top of it," i.e., C-
G-A treated motivically, as in the theme of the first movement; re-
arrangements of *pns*, as in the sixth movement, the theme of which
does not include a fifth or even its inversion, a fourth, as a melodic
interval (Example 7.15, measures 1–2); further variants of the original motif, with other notes interpolated—for example, the opening
theme of the third movement, which begins not with *pns* but with p^2s
or p^2s^2 (Example 7.16A, equivalent to sc 3-9 [027] or 4-22 [0247]); and
themes whose contours resemble those of earlier themes—for example, the opening theme of the fourth movement (Example 7.16B),
which though it resembles the second movement theme (Example
7.14A) has no major second, and belongs not to *pns* but to M^3 (sc 4-19
[0148]). There is also a "closing theme" that appears in the second
movement and is heard again shortly before the end of the fourth
and the sixth movements (Example 7.16C), which belongs to the
sonority p^3d^2 (sc 5-14 [01257]), has no special kinship to *pns,* and is
without either a fifth or major second in the melody (although if the
C♮ in the melody is ignored as a "passing tone," the melody would
form *pns*). Clearly, the kind of set-class consistency that analysts
have found in sections of "freely atonal" twentieth-century pieces by
Bartók, Schoenberg, and Stravinsky is lacking in this piece.

Example 7.16A   Hanson, Symphony no. 6, III, mm. 1–3

Example 7.16B   Hanson, Symphony no. 6, IV, m. 1

Example 7.16C   Hanson, Symphony no. 6, II, mm. 4–5 before rehearsal 16

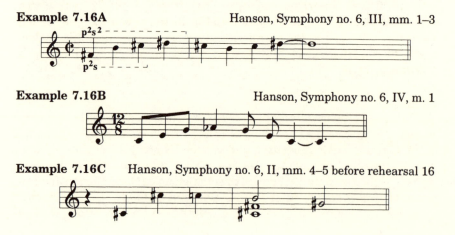

In search of more consistent results, we may also look briefly at Hanson's *Mosaics*, a theme-and-variations for orchestra that, like the Symphony no. 6, is colorful and effectively scored, with sharp contrasts and a brooding, massive power. Hanson felt that this piece showed the influence of the theory "probably more than anything else . . . except *For the First Time* of course."[210] A page of sketches for this piece shows the main theme (Example 7.17), beneath which are the pitch names E-G-G♯-B-C and, below that, the interval succession in integers (3-1-3-1), which clearly indicates the sonority M^4 (with interval analysis $p^2m^4n^2d^2$, sc 5-21 [01458]).[211] On the liner notes to his recording of this piece, Hanson says that it "might be called a variation on the relationship of the major third, the minor third, and the minor second," and the M^4 sonority does contain all three of these intervals.[212]

Example 7.17   Hanson, *Mosaics*, mm. 1–10

It is also true that the further exposition of the theme (between rehearsal number 1 and rehearsal 5) utilizes operations of expansion and contraction consistent with the "modulation" of sonorities. But after this section, there is little or no consistency. Much of the remainder of the piece is dominated by diatonic or modal scales, by parallel triads over pedal tones (as in the *Sinfonia Sacra*), or by new and unrelated sonorities (such as *pns*, or sc 3-7 [025], in the fifth variation and *nsd/n*, or sc 5-10 [01346], in the seventh). The second variation, for example, seems clearly based upon diatonic inflections of E, since it clearly begins in E major, with perhaps a Phrygian inflection:

Example 7.18   Hanson, *Mosaics*, m. 2 after rehearsal 9

In short, we see a situation much like that of the Symphony no. 6: Hanson's statement that this piece is "a variation on the relationship of the major third, the minor third, and the minor second" can be taken as accurate only in the loosest sense, not in a way consistent with a thorough application of the theory.

And so, having examined a number of late pieces of Hanson's, we are led to the surprising but inescapable conclusion that the works he considered to be strongly influenced by his theory differ little in their fundamental materials and organization from works he considered to have little or no influence (or from those about which he made no comment). In fact, there is a much greater divergence in compositional technique between even the "strongly influenced" works, such as the Symphony no. 6, and the two demonstration pieces examined in the previous chapter. Whereas in the demosntration pieces the melodic and harmonic material is consistently derived from a predetermined sonority, in the other pieces there is little consistency of sonority in either melodic or harmonic material; and even where Hanson's sketches make clear that he is using, and thinking in terms of, a sonority from *Harmonic Materials*, it is not used consistently.

But if these findings seem to be perplexing or contradictory, several of Hanson's comments about his characteristic methods of composition may shed some light. At one point during their 1978 interviews, Hanson's former student asked him if he had ever "fallen back" on his system to get musical ideas when starting a new piece. Hanson replied:

> Yes, I think every composer does that to some extent; it is technically known as priming the pump! . . . [A]fter you're pretty well drained of ideas, you almost have to go to the well to get replenished. . . . I don't mean to imply that I do that all the time, but it's one way of spurring your imagination because it does get you out of set tone patterns, the major scale or minor scale or the modal scale.[213]

He went on to say that he had recently begun the clarinet Fantasy (which became part of *Nymph and Satyr)* in such a manner, after having been "depleted" by writing *A Sea Symphony*. This remark and similar ones show that such playing with characteristic intervals was, if not an everyday practice with Hanson, then an habitual one, in the same way that other composers improvise at the piano for inspiration. (Hanson said that he himself did not use the piano while creating, because "you rely too much on what you can actually play, and there are many ideas you have you can't begin to play.")[214]

Hanson's sketchbooks and miscellaneous sketches provide additional illumination on this habit of "priming the pump." Mention has already been made of the projection notations in the sketch for the *Elegy*. Another example can be found on the verso of a page of piano-score sketches for the first movement of his 1948 Concerto for Piano and Orchestra, on which can be found sketches of scales going upward from middle C with different inflections of scale degrees. One of these scales has several possible interval successions indicated (in integers) below it, each one corresponding to a different set of inflections of the third, fourth, sixth and seventh scale degrees; and to the right of it is a column containing a group of symbols from the second stage of the theory's development (a-B-c-c), although to what this column refers is unclear. Also on this page is notated a series of simultaneities that clearly shows a relationship to various types of projection as mentioned in *Harmonic Materials*. (See Example 7.19; the numerical labels at the bottom have been added by the author.)[215] Sonorities #1 and #2 are projections of the perfect fifth; #3 shows a "projection by involution" of fifths and minor thirds above and below G, and #4 a projection of fifths and major thirds above and below.[216] Sonorities #5 and #6 show the addition of a single foreign tone to the projection of two fifths; #7 through #10 show the projection of fifths at the intervals of the major third, the minor third, the minor second, and the tritone, respectively. Below the staff shown in Example 7.19, the sketch has several bass clef chords that are transpositions of these sonorities, including (beneath number 5) a chord that reads upward Bb-F-B-C, and below it "1 1 5 5," which is the interval succession of this sonority, when rearranged as Bb-B-C-F.

Example 7.19   Hanson, Piano Concerto, sketch (facsimile)

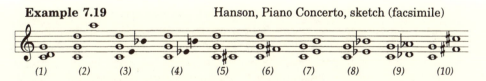

It should be added that of the nondiatonic sonorities in this list (# 4, 5, 6, 9 and 10), none seems to be a prominent feature of the Piano Concerto. But as mentioned in the fourth chapter of this book, similar sketches can be found in many music notebooks and sheets of music paper used by Hanson for pieces from various periods. Sometimes these sketches show sonorities that appear in the piece on which he was working; sometimes, as with the Piano Concerto, they seem to have little or no connection. Many of the projection sketches made prior to the publication of *Harmonic Materials* in 1960 may have been part of Hanson's developmental work on the theory, representing an occasional break from composition to tackle a particular problem. But curiously enough, Hanson continued to sketch out such projections even after the book was published. In a considerable number of his music notebooks from the 1960s, some pages have sketches for a particular piece, and other pages are covered with sketches of various projections.

All of this projection writing may appear puzzling at first, because it seems unnecessary. Once the theory had been finished and published, there was no need for Hanson to continue to sketch out projections, when by referring to *Harmonic Materials* he could find every possible sonority and simply transpose or invert the ones in which he was interested. It is possible that some of this work represented Hanson's attempts to correct errors that he had found in his theory.[217] But, as his comment about "priming the pump" suggests, it may also be that he found the activity of writing out projections to be a useful aid to composition, in and of itself.

For instance, there are several small spiral-bound notebooks from the mid-1960s that contain both sketches for the Symphony no. 6 and sketches of projections. One of these notebooks, labelled "Sketch – Symphony no. VI – Vol. I," includes sketches for the fifth movement that start on a verso page and continue on the next verso, while on the two recto pages is an alternate opening (presumably for the same movement) based on a very literal perfect-fifth projection.[218] (Hanson did not use this in the Symphony no. 6, but as we have already seen, his seventh symphony has a very similar opening.) There are other such notebooks, such as the one titled "Harmonic Projections 1964," that are filled with projections, over some of which Hanson has written "OK."[219] This suggests that when inspiration ran dry, he found it therapeutic or inspirational to take a break from the composition sketch and write out a large number of projections—perhaps expansions of a sonority he was already using in the piece, or perhaps simply at random—and he would then select from these a few that seemed appropriate or pleasing.

We have already made note of Hanson's admonition that his theory is not meant as a "method" nor "system" of composition, but "a compendium of harmonic-melodic material," and his expressed hope "that this volume may serve the composer in much the same way that a dictionary or thesaurus serves the author."[220] From these, from the notations on his sketches, and from his remarks on "priming the pump," it becomes clear that when composing—except in the two demonstration pieces—for the most part Hanson used the vast apparatus of his theory simply as a starting point, a source. Projecting sonorities was a method for prompting musical ideas when they were not otherwise flowing, and sometimes for developing small ideas into larger ones—but only to the extent that he felt was necessary in a particular piece, without any special regard for rigor or consistency. This would explain why *Mosaics* and the Symphony no. 6 are no more consistent in their intervallic relations than are the other pieces examined in this chapter, and why even works that Hanson thought to be uninfluenced by the theory have some elements of interval projection.

So we find that only the two "demonstration pieces" show a relatively thorough and consistent application of the theory in their composition. It must be added, however, that these pieces are not the best arguments for a consistent use of the theory. Despite its craft, *For the First Time* never quite escapes its origins as a set of comparatively easy pedagogical pieces for children. As most of its reviewers agreed, it is light and pleasant but unmemorable.[221] Whether because Hanson felt it necessary to present the basic sonority prominently at the beginning of each movement (usually in the form of arpeggios or scales), resulting in melodic material with little distinctive contour, or because he was unable or unwilling to summon up the inspiration, these little pieces never rise above the status of *Gebrauchsmusik*. Nor is there any attempt to forge a musical unity. There is no connection among the movements, except between "Clowns" and "Dance," which share the melodic gesture of rising triads in triple rhythm; and precisely because this instance is unique, it raises the suspicion of having been coincidental. The only other suggestion of an overall conception is the simple alteration of slow and fast movements (again with the exception of the *Allegretto* "Clowns" being followed by the *Allegro con brio* "Dance," so that the suite both begins and ends with slow movements); and beyond the use of different sonorities for different movements, the theory seems to play no part in higher levels of musical organization. It is perhaps indicative of the work's failure to arouse much interest in either performers or listeners that, as of this point, Hanson's own recording is the only commercial one that has been made of the orchestral version in the forty years since he finished it, and that the first commercial recording of the piano version did not appear until thirty years after it was published.[222]

As for *Young Person's Guide to the Six-Tone Scale,* as striking and diverse as most of the movements are, they are all too short to make any lasting impression. The result for the listener is an effect of many beautiful fragments but no coherent totality. If there is an inherent risk in any suite or long set of variations that at the end the parts may not add up to a whole, then a suite with no central theme and thirty-five movements, each extremely short and in a different tempo and mood from the previous one, makes the risk much worse. It seems a pity that Hanson did not in fact utilize an actual theme for his "variations." While the demands of the various six-tone sonorities would have deformed any theme almost beyond recognition, it would have been an interesting compositional challenge to show a theme undergoing progressively greater transformations. It would certainly have helped to provide the unity that is sorely lacking, and might also have necessitated an ordering of the movements that would have seemed more logical to a listener than the one used by Hanson. Despite the superficially systematic grouping of the movements according to their predominant intervals, his habit of separating sonorities into alternating triads makes most of the movements sound, to some extent, as though they have a triadic basis, which to a large extent vitiates a sense of intensification or consistent harmonic change. (Another possibility would have been to group movements with the same predominant intervals together into sections with common tempi and moods, so that instead of thirty-five tiny movements there could have been seven substantial sections.) Nor did Hanson help the situation by fashioning relatively stable endings for most of the movements; the many little stops preclude whatever momentum he might have otherwise established. In particular the end of movement #33, which is fast and loud and, like the beginning movement, C-centric, sounds as though it is the end of the work as a whole. Like *For the First Time, Young Person's Guide to the Six-Tone Scale* remains one of Hanson's most obscure pieces.[223] As of this writing, it has had no recordings since its first one; the first recording has never been reissued on compact disc, and the piece was not even published until 1995, twenty-three years after its completion.

Another possible reason for the lack of popularity of both "demonstration pieces" is that in writing them Hanson had to deny himself the full use of two of his greatest strengths: rich pungent harmonies imbued with Romantic intensity, and strongly defined, memorable themes. (In both *For the First Time* and *Young Person's Guide,* much of the melodic material appears as either arpeggiation or scales, although the melodic contours tend to be stronger in the later work.) It could be said that he nevertheless succeeded to some extent in supplying the rich harmonies, especially in *Young Person's Guide.* As for the undoubted deficiency of distinctive melodies, it is hard to say how much of it was inherent in his self-imposed assignments, and how much might have been different had he not from the beginning considered *For the First Time* "a stunt" and *Young Person's Guide* "a kind of joke."[224]

In any case, the relative obscurity of these pieces suggests strongly that Hanson's inclination, in the majority of his compositions, to rely upon inspiration rather than upon a consistent application of the theory was artistically a wise one. Based on his own words, it would seem that Hanson felt this way himself.

> When my instinct tells me that I want to go the other way [from adherence to a projection], I'd go the other way, regardless of whether I'm going against my own series or not.

> I think there is a basic difference in the approach of the scientific mind and the creative mind. . . . I think the analytic mind can be of help to the creative mind . . . but I think that as soon as your major interest becomes the diagram of the work or the mathematical relations within a work . . . you are missing your calling. . . . Composition must be a certain free flow of fantasy that doesn't have anything to do with a preconceived system.[225]

> I am a "natural" composer. I write music because I have to write. Though I have a profound interest in theoretical problems, my own music comes "from the heart" and is a direct expression of my own emotional reactions.[226]

Chapter 8

Coda: The Elements of Style

As we have seen, the question of the influence of Howard Hanson's theory upon his later compositions does not have a simple answer. With the exception of *For the First Time* and *Young Person's Guide to the Six-Tone Scale*—and regardless of whether, from his own perspective, the influence of the theory had been strong or had been nonexistent—his use of the theory in his compositions was in fact neither fundamental nor consistent.

But this conclusion raises additional questions of its own. First, given that the theory had some degree of influence on most of his later pieces and on his compositional methods, can we gauge the influence of the theory on his style in general?

As mentioned in the brief discussion in Chapter 2, the common critical perspective on Hanson's style is that his music, at least in the better-known early pieces such as the Symphony no. 1, Symphony no. 2, and *Merry Mount* Suite, is full of long, lyrical melodies and lush harmonies, often based on extended tertian structures. An early appreciation of Hanson's music refers to his frequent employment of "lush melody . . . unabashed in its sentiment . . . with an accompaniment of rich, pulsating harmonies."[227] Other typical characterizations of his music note "a strongly appealing score, gushing with warm melody"; or they refer to "broad, sonorous, sometimes lyric melody"; to "outspokenly romantic . . . broadly arched melodies" and "full, richly orchestrated texture"; to "the peculiarly American spaciousness of his melodic structures"; and to "broadly lyrical" or "broad, flowing, diatonic" themes and "sonorous harmonies."[228]

As was also mentioned in Chapter 2, writers who are familiar with more than the usual handful of Hanson's works have noted a general change in style between these early works and his later ones, with the change generally assumed to have occurred at some point during the 1940s. The style of the later works is usually said to differ from the earlier style in that there are fewer lyrical melodies as such, with even large-scale works mostly built up from short motivic cells or from small groups of characteristic intervals presented as scales or arpeggios. There are also said to be far fewer traditionally Romantic, tertian-based harmonies. A review of an early performance of his Piano Concerto says, "We had become so accustomed to the long melodic lines in Dr. Hanson's earlier compositions that it came as somewhat of a shock when we heard only short thematic fragments in the new work."[229] Similarly, another writer says of Hanson's Symphony no. 4 that it "departs from the Romanticism of Hanson's early works"; a later chronicle asserts that "as the years went by he tempered the somewhat facile sentimentalism" of his early works, "and employed more and more of the new resources of contemporary music"; and another refers to the tendency in Hanson's later works "towards greater economy of material and more compact form."[230]

It would seem reasonable to attribute such changes, at least in part, to the influence of the theory. The use of short motivic cells rather than extended themes can be safely said to characterize most, if not all, of Hanson's later works—such as *For the First Time*, *Sinfonia Sacra*, the *Elegy*, Symphony no. 6, and even *A Sea Symphony*—and it seems quite plausible that this might be, to some extent, a result of Hanson's years of intensive work exploring the relations of tonal structures and the repeated superimpositions of characteristic intervals and sonorities. (It would be more difficult to say whether this putative influence of the theory on Hanson's style was due primarily to his having spent so much time thinking about it, or to an increasing need to "prime the pump" because of a declining inspiration.)

On the other hand, it could also be said with some validity that this stylistic change in Hanson's music was essentially an illusion, and that even in his early works, many of the most characteristic melodies are not as broad, lyrical and long-lined as they seem to the critics. For proof we may examine from a melodic viewpoint three of the best-known themes of Hanson's early period: the second theme from the slow movement of the *"Nordic"* Symphony no. 1, the famous second theme from the *"Romantic"* Symphony no. 2, and the theme from the Love Duet movement of the *Merry Mount* Suite.

The theme from the Symphony no. 1 is shown as Example 8.1. In terms of thematic construction, the entire melody is built from only two motifs, labelled *a* and *b* in the example. In addition, *b* could be considered to be only a slight extension of the inversion of *a*, so in essence the entire theme could be said to be built from the *a* motif.

Example 8.1   Hanson, Symphony no. 1, II, rehearsal D

The theme from the Symphony no. 2 is shown as Example 8.2. This melody is constructed from three motifs, labelled *c*, *d*, and *e*. However, *c* is simply the threefold repetition of a note, and *e* is clearly a variant of the inversion of *d*.

Example 8.2   Hanson, Symphony no. 2, I, rehearsal F

The first theme of the third movement of the *Merry Mount* Suite is shown as Example 8.3A.[231] This entire theme is built from a single motif *f*. The second theme, shown as Example 8.3B, adds a second motif *g*, which also recurs frequently, either transposed or inverted. (Curiously enough, motif *f* in Example 8.3A is very similar to motif *d* in Example 8.2, and to the inversion of motif *a* in Example 8.1. But to explore Hanson's apparent fixation on such scalar three-note motifs at this period in his career would take us too far afield.)

Example 8.3A   Hanson, *Merry Mount* Suite, III, mm. 1–6

Largamente, molto espressivo

Example 8.3B   Hanson, *Merry Mount* Suite, III, rehearsal 203

con passione

What we can see clearly in the above examples are not the "broadly arched," "long melodic lines" that are supposed to be characteristic of Hanson's early period, but themes that have been constructed from the virtually obsessive repetition, transposition and inversion of one or two short motifs. Of course, there are other early Hanson themes that are indeed "broad, flowing," and "spacious," but the above examples are representative of much of the thematic material in the major works of this period. In contrast to the standard critical perspective, it would be more accurate to say that while there are differences between the melodic structures of the early works and those of the later works, these differences are not so much of kind as of degree. Not counting some very early pieces written before he went to Rome, Hanson's melodic style did not change greatly over the course of his entire career.

This new perspective, of course, is not the whole story. As mentioned in Chapter 2, Hanson's harmonic practice did evolve from the use of rich, full tertian chords and traditional functional tonality that underlie all three of the above melodies, to more spare and dissonant, less triadic structures, with little or no functional harmony even by implication. Even in this area, though, the evolution was less drastic than it appears. While the harmonies and textures of the *"Nordic"* Symphony (from 1923) still show an influence of late Romantics such as Tchaikovsky and Dvorak, the *"Romantic"* Symphony (from 1930) is already considerably more original and "modern." As James E. Perone points out, "Even the sometimes narrowly-defined Symphony no. 2 finds Hanson making use of quartal structures melodically and harmonically, dissonant bitonal chords, and one rather overt reference to the blues scale in a transitional theme."[232] Thus even the evolution of Hanson's harmonic practice, while clearly perceptible, was nevertheless smaller and more gradual than the standard conception would suggest.

But our revised conception leads us inevitably to another question. Now that we have an idea of the influence of Hanson's theory upon his music, we may also ask the converse: What influence did Hanson's music have upon his theory? In other words, did Hanson's characteristic techniques and style of composition have something to do with his developing such a theory in the first place?

Indeed, we might well ask what led an active composer, who was also an busy teacher, college administrator, and conductor, to spend years working on a theory. An interest in theory is not unusual for a composer, of course; in the twentieth century, many composers were keenly interested in such matters. In Hanson's case, though, a composer felt compelled not only to ponder the questions of interval relationships, but also to develop a comprehensive system to classify them all. As discussed in Chapter 4, to some extent such ideas seem to have been in the air. The question remains, however, whether there was something in Hanson's own personality, or in his compositional style and method, that led to his choosing to spend years working in the area of interval relations, as opposed (for instance) to rhythm, or voice-leading.

We have seen that, from an early age, Hanson had been interested in the application of new scientific principles and inventions to musical problems. This led to such results as a machine for analyzing the formant distribution of singing voices, a machine for showing overtones optically, tests for measuring musical talent, and tests for measuring the emotional effects of different harmonies. It also led to the magazine article in which he insisted that the theorist should be "a pioneer" and investigate "nature's laws." We have seen that late in life, in response to a question about whether he had "done some fooling around" with the theory before he began to use it in his classes, he said, "I think I've been fooling around with it all my life, really." He added that he had always been interested in intervals as compositional elements, and several times he referred to his long-standing conviction that "Melody grows out of harmony, and harmony grows out of melody. . . . I think if I have one major tenet in composition, that is it: that there *is* no difference between so-called vertical and horizontal. . . . And I was always fascinated by how much logic there is in musical progression."[233]

We have also seen that it was not unusual for Hanson, throughout his career, to construct themes from the repetition, transposition or inversion of one or two germ motifs or intervals. In fact, he thought of his music as being dominated by different intervals at different periods:

There was a long period where I was a perfect-fifth composer. This goes back to *Beowulf*; it's certainly not perfect

fifth music by any means, but the basis is the perfect fifth.
Later on, I think I became probably mostly interested in
combinations of the major third and major second.[234]

When his interviewer suggested that Hanson's Symphony no. 3 was
"very heavy" with thirds, Hanson agreed.[235]
   A survey of the main themes of this symphony bears out Hanson's remarks, within limits. See Examples 8.4A–8.4H.

Example 8.4A   Hanson, Symphony no. 3, I, m. 1

Example 8.4B   Hanson, Symphony no. 3, I, mm. 5–6 after rehearsal 2

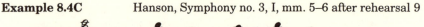

Example 8.4C   Hanson, Symphony no. 3, I, mm. 5–6 after rehearsal 9

Example 8.4D   Hanson, Symphony no. 3, I, mm. 3–4 after rehearsal 13

Example 8.4E   Hanson, Symphony no. 3, I, mm. 1–2 after rehearsal 17

Example 8.4F   Hanson, Symphony no. 3, II, mm. 2–4 before rehearsal 1

Example 8.4G   Hanson, Symphony no. 3, III, m. 1 before–4 after rehearsal 5

Example 8.4H   Hanson, Symphony no. 3, IV, mm. 1–2 after rehearsal 5

These themes show a considerable, though not unusual, use of thirds in the melodies and contours of Examples 8.4A, 8.4C, 8.4D, 8.4E, and 8.4F, in the bass of 8.4B and in the accompaniments of 8.4D and 8.4F. (The first and second movements also end on sustained thirds.) In addition, scalar passages of parallel thirds are prevalent throughout the symphony. Examples 8.5A through 8.5D show characteristic examples from each movement.

Example 8.5A   Hanson, Symphony no. 3, I, mm. 4–5 after rehearsal 3

Example 8.5B   Hanson, Symphony no. 3, II, mm. 3–4 after rehearsal 12

Example 8.5C   Hanson, Symphony no. 3, III, mm. 1–2 after rehearsal 10

Example 8.5D   Hanson, Symphony no. 3, IV, mm. 1–2 after rehearsal 20

It may be noted that these thirds are both major and minor thirds. They are consistent only with the traditionally generic idea of "thirds," not with the more rigorous notion of a distinction between *n* and *m*, i.e., between three and four semitones. (The reader may recall Hanson's original, abandoned symbology for the theory, mentioned at the end of the fourth chapter of this book, in which the single symbol *b* stood for both minor and major thirds.)

Nevertheless, the fact that Hanson considered himself, at various times, a "perfect-fifth composer" or "major-third composer" is in itself revelatory about his lifelong perspective on intervals and their relation to composition. He considered Ravel largely a minor-third composer, and when asked about Stravinsky he replied categorically, "PDT!—Perfect fifth, tritone, and minor second."[236] Hence it is not unnatural that he would have tended to think in terms of characteristic intervals and pitch collections as the basis for composition—his own or that of others.

One last piece of evidence that this was habitual, even in Hanson's earlier music, can be found in the first movement of his Symphony no. 2, the first theme group of which is shown in Examples 8.6A through 8.6C. According to Hanson the opening sonority, Example 8.6A, is based on the bitonal combination of major triads a tritone apart (D♭ and G).[237] But the melody of Example 8.6B, a short fanfare-like motif, is entirely based on the perfect fourth, an interval that plays a prominent part throughout the symphony in both melody and harmony. The fourth is also an important element of later themes—for instance in the quarter-note triplet in the lower staff at the end of Example 8.6C. (The melody in the lower staff of Example 8.6C essentially fulfills the function of the first theme of the movement.)

Hanson's fascination with intervals is underscored by a small discrepancy between the final score and a composition sketch in one of the three music notebooks used by Hanson for sketching the symphony, one for each movement.[238] Example 8.7A is a transcription from the sketch of the first movement; Example 8.7B is a reduction

Example 8.6A   Hanson, Symphony no. 2, I, m. 1

Example 8.6B   Hanson, Symphony no. 2, I, mm. 3–5 after rehearsal A

Example 8.6C   Hanson, Symphony no. 2, I, mm. 8–12 after rehearsal A

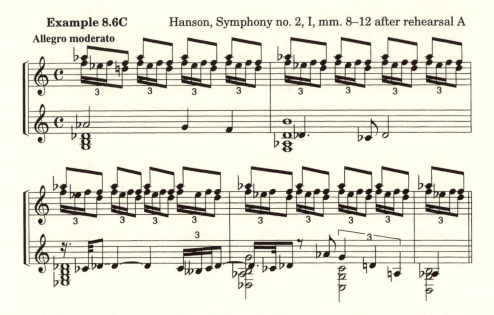

of the corresponding place in the final score. This passage, like much of the work, is saturated with the interval of the fourth. Fourths can be found not only in the woodwind countermelody, but also in the quartal accompaniment and the trumpet countermelody, which (in the sketch) uses the same pitch classes as the upper line of the woodwinds. (The primary melody of this passage is actually in the violins, which at this point are sustaining the final high C♯ of the melody over the accompanimental chord.) Although the sketch uses two measures of 2/4 instead of one measure of 4/4, and omits the triplet brackets, and although there are minor differences in register and doubling, the sketch and score are essentially identical, with one important exception. The one significant difference is the change in pitch of the third dyad of each triplet in the upper staff. Ultimately Hanson decided on a downward leap of a fifth to the third dyad—perhaps because, with the second triplet now in the same octave as the first rather than in a lower octave, the first dyad of each triplet becomes an octave-displaced repetition of the third dyad of the previous triplet. But it is characteristic of his lifelong fascination with the superimposition and saturation of intervals that the original downward leap from the second to the third dyad in each triplet, like the leap from the first to the second dyad, was yet another fourth.

Although Hanson went on to refine and codify his theoretical preoccupations into a complex and comprehensive system, we can see that between his theory and his practice the influence went both ways—or rather, that both theory and practice were parts of a recipro-

Example 8.7A   Hanson, Symphony no. 2, I, sketch

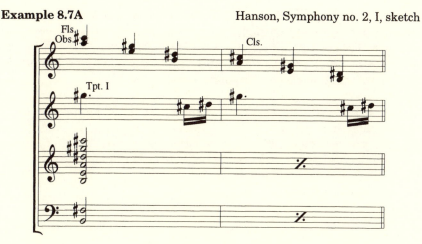

Example 8.7B   Hanson, Symphony no. 2, I, m. 3 before rehearsal C

cal process in which his predilections in each area reinforced and further extended his work in the other. Just as, once he had developed his theoretical system, it consciously or unconsciously exerted varying degrees of influence on virtually everything he composed, so it could also be said that he was led to make an exhaustive study of interval relationships precisely because the exhaustive exploitation of those relationships had always been an important part of his compositional method and—perhaps just as importantly—of his own perception of his method.

Hanson always insisted that the theoretical and the creative aspects of music be taught and studied together, because they were two sides of the same discipline. Thus, at the end of a long career, this composer could feel justified in saying that he had been working on a theory for his entire lifetime. For Howard Hanson, the theory and practice of music were inextricably intertwined, two essential and complementary aspects of a single vocation:

> a part of infinity itself. It is tangible, it is intangible. It is science, it is art. It is emotion, it is intellect. . . . It calls for our deepest emotional development, the greatest use of our intellectual powers, and a supreme devotion to beauty.[239]

Appendix A:
Hanson's Master Diagram

Howard Hanson, *Harmonic Materials of Modern Music*, foldout insert

The body of the Appendix appears on the following two pages.

From Howard Hanson, *Harmonic Materials of Modern Music*

Copyright © 1960 by

Appleton-Century-Crofts, Inc.

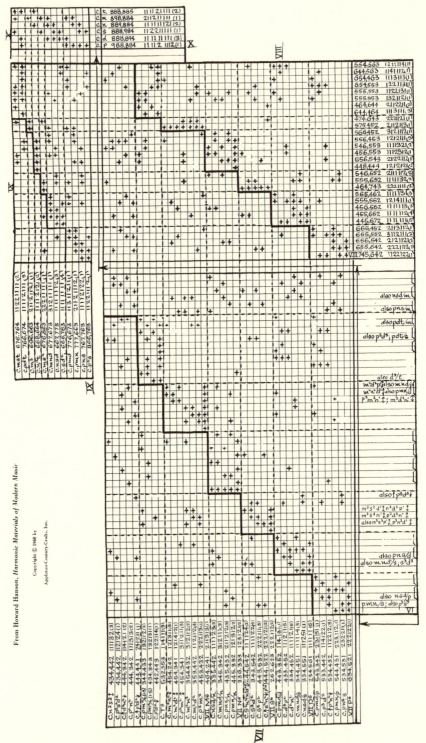

146

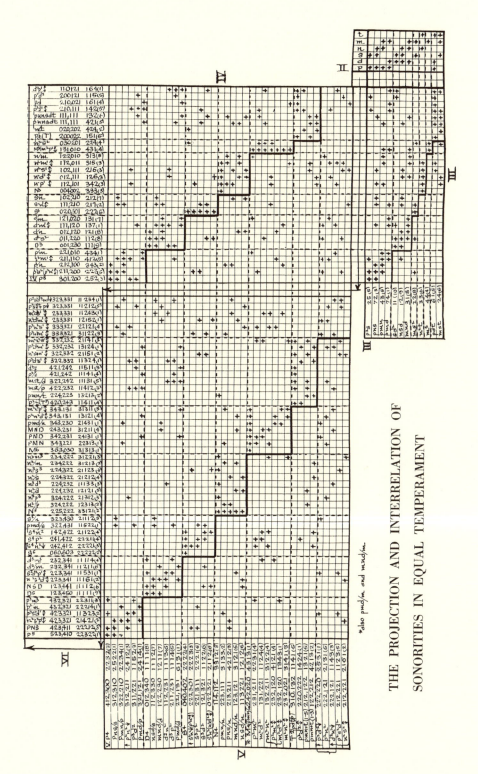

THE PROJECTION AND INTERRELATION OF
SONORITIES IN EQUAL TEMPERAMENT

Appendix B:
Sample Page from Chapter 50 of
Harmonic Materials

Howard Hanson, *Harmonic Materials of Modern Music*,
page 357

The body of the Appendix appears on the following page.

EXAMPLE 50-1

Appendix C:
For the First Time, "Dreams"

piano version

The body of the Appendix appears on the following three pages.

Appendix D:
Young Person's Guide to the Six-Tone Scale, #34

The body of the Appendix appears on the following page.

[In this excerpt, the original sonority is labelled
O; its involution is OI; its isomeric twin is T;
and the involution of the twin is TI.]

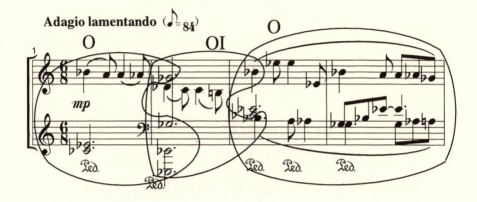

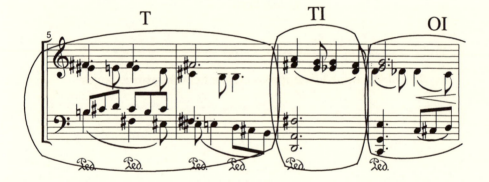

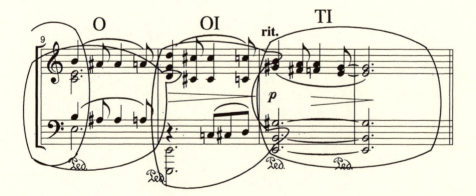

Appendix E:
Young Person's Guide
to the Six-Tone Scale, #35

reduction

The body of the Appendix appears on the following three pages.

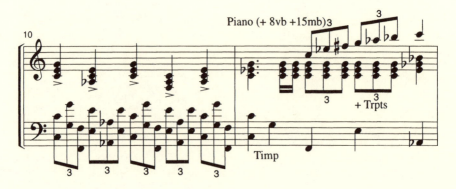

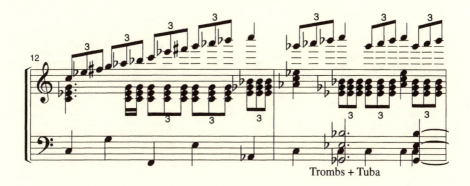

Trombs + Tuba

ff

Clars

mf + Piano, Bs Cl, Bsns 8vb

Piano, Fl (Picc 8va)

8va

Eng Hn

mf

Brass, Bsns, Bs Cl

Appendix F:
Symphony no. 6,
First Movement

reduction

The body of the Appendix appears on the following three pages.

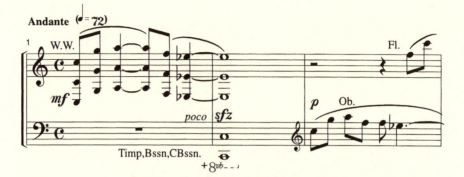

Appendix G:
The Major-Second Projection

**Howard Hanson, *Harmonic Materials of Modern Music*,
page 278**

The body of the Appendix appears on the following page.

EXAMPLE 41-3

Appendix H:
The *pns* Projection

Howard Hanson, *Harmonic Materials of Modern Music*, pages 288–89

The body of the Appendix appears on the following page.

Notes

CHAPTER 1
INTRODUCTION

1. Howard Hanson, *Harmonic Materials of Modern Music: Resources of the Tempered Scale* (New York: Appleton-Century-Crofts, 1960).

2. David Russell Williams, *Conversations with Howard Hanson* (Arkadelphia, Ark.: Delta Publications, 1988), 7, 40.

3. Most of Howard Hanson's extant manuscripts and sketches can be found in the Howard Hanson Papers, Accession no. 997.12, Eastman School of Music Archives, Sibley Library, Eastman School of Music, University of Rochester, Rochester, New York. Also see Marilyn V. Plain, *Howard Hanson: A Comprehensive Catalog of the Manuscripts* (Rochester: Eastman School of Music Press, 1997).

4. As will be discussed in Chapter 4, the only substantial exception to this lack of acknowledgment is Robert Sutton's article "Howard Hanson, Set Theory Pioneer," *Sonus* 8 (1987): 17–39, which deals with the chronological relation between *Harmonic Materials* and similar theoretical writings by Allen Forte, Donald Martino, George Perle, and David Lewin. Shorter and somewhat dismissive surveys of Hanson's contributions to music theory can be found in Janet Schmalfeldt, *Berg's "Wozzeck": Harmonic Language and Dramatic Design* (New Haven: Yale University Press, 1983), 9–11, and in Jonathan W. Bernard, "Chord, Collection, and Set in Twentieth-Century Theory," in *Music Theory in Concept and Practice*, edited by James M. Baker, David W. Beach, and Jonathan W. Bernard (Rochester: University of Rochester Press, 1997), 45–49; these will also be discussed in Chapter 4.

5. See Bernard, "Chord, Collection, and Set in Twentieth-Century Theory," 48, note 77.

6. Hanson's written and recorded comments include the liner notes for the long-playing records *The Composer and His Orchestra Vol. II: An Analysis, with Musical Illustrations, of Howard Hanson's "Mosaics"* (Mercury Records MG50267, 1962); *The Composer and His Orchestra Vol. III: An Analysis, with Musical Illustrations, of Howard Hanson's "For the First Time"* (Mercury Records MG50357 & SR90357, 1963); and *Young Composer's Guide to the Six Tone Scale* (Mercury Golden Imports SRI 75132, 1978). The apparent discrepancy between this latter title and the title used in the text (*Young Person's Guide to the Six-Tone Scale*) is due to Hanson's having apparently changed his mind about the title after the recording was issued, as will be discussed in Chapter 6.

CHAPTER 2
THE BACKGROUND: HANSON'S LIFE AND CAREER

7. Quotes from Howard Hanson, "The Scope of the Music Education Program," *Music Educators Journal* 34 (June–July 1948): 57; "Howard Hanson on Music," *Howard Hanson: A Tribute* (Eastman School of Music souvenir program, 28 October 1981); and Howard Hanson, "The Place of Creative Arts," *Vital Speeches of the Day* 30 (1963): 90.

8. See Robert C. Monroe, "Howard Hanson: American Music Educator" (Ph.D. diss., Florida State University, 1970), 15. Luther College later merged with Midland College and became Midland Lutheran College, now located in Fremont, Nebraska.

9. See Andrea Sherlock Kalyn, "Constructing a Nation's Music: Howard Hanson's American Composers' Concerts and Festivals of American Music, 1925–71" (Ph.D. diss, University of Rochester, 2001), 51.

10. David Russell Williams, *Conversations with Howard Hanson* (Arkadelphia, Ark.: Delta Publications, 1988), 22.

11. John Brzustowicz, telephone conversation with the author, 3 December 2002. Brzustowicz grew up next door to the Hansons in Rochester and spent much time with Hanson there and elsewhere. He has in his possession a large archive of Howard Hanson's personal papers and items, including an unpublished autobiography written during the years 1965–71, personal and business letters, notebooks, autograph manuscripts, and memorabilia. Unfortunately, because of the disorganized state of these materials, and because of other problems in obtaining access to them that cannot be discussed here, I was unable to examine more than a fraction of them for this book.

12. "Inventions New and Interesting: Singing into a Tin Can to Test the Voice," *Scientific American* 117 (22 September 1917): 212; Marjory M. Fisher, "Studying the Physical Aspect of Overtones," *Musical America* 30 (23 August 1919): 29. According to John Brzustowicz, the formant analyzer was actually

built to Hanson's specifications by a tinsmith in Wahoo (letter to the author, 16 January 2003).

13. Howard Hanson, "The Indictment Against the Musical Theorist," *Musical America* 27 (5 January 1918): 35.

14. Marjory M. Fisher, "Measuring Musical Talent," *Musical America* 28 (17 August 1918): 13; "Psychological Reaction to Isolated Chords Shown by Pacific Coast Musician's Tests," *Musical America* 33 (5 March 1921): 45.

15. See Kalyn, "Constructing a Nation's Music," 238–39.

16. Williams, *Conversations with Howard Hanson*, 13–14.

17. Kalyn, "Constructing a Nation's Music," 81.

18. Hamilton B. Allen, "At 70, Howard Hanson Looks Mostly Forward," *Rochester Times-Union,* 29 October 1966, section C: 4.

19. Nicolas Slonimsky, *Baker's Biographical Dictionary of Musicians* (New York: Schirmer Books, Macmillan, Inc., 1992), 715.

20. Hanson, letter to Rush Rhees, 26 January 1924, quoted in Kalyn, "Constructing a Nation's Music," 93. For much of the information summarized in the following section I am indebted to Monroe, "Howard Hanson: American Music Educator"; to Kalyn, "Constructing a Nation's Music"; to Howard Hanson, *A Decade of Progress* (Rochester: University of Rochester, 1931); to Charles Riker, *The Eastman School of Music: Its First Quarter Century, 1921–1946* (Rochester: University of Rochester, 1948); and to telephone conversations with present and former Eastman faculty members Robert Morris (19 November 2001), Vincent Lenti (21 January 2002), John Beck (25 January 2002), William Francis McBeth (25 January 2002 and 18 March 2003), David Russell Williams (25 January 2002), Robert Gauldin (21 April 2002), and Ruth T. Watanabe (15 May 2002).

21. For more on the changing attitudes of Hanson and other American musicians toward European models, see the first chapter of Kalyn, "Constructing a Nation's Music."

22. Howard Hanson, Letter to the President of the University of Rochester, n.d. (1934?), 3. This can be found in the Volume 7 Scrapbook of press clippings in the Howard Hanson Papers. See the citation for the Howard Hanson Papers in the Bibliography.

23. Eastman School of Music, *Official Bulletin* (February 1964): 23.

24. Paul Henry Lang, "From the Mail Pouch: Professor Opposes Insistence on Degrees For Teaching Music in Universities," *New York Times*, 1 November 1953, section X: 9; Howard Hanson, "Mail Pouch: Dispute Over Degrees," *New York Times*, 8 November 1953, section X: 7.

25. Howard Hanson, "Professional Music Education in the United States," *Musical Courier* 151 (1955): 64; quoted in "Howard Hanson (1896–1981)," *The Instrumentalist* 35 (1981): 102–03.

26. Howard Hanson, "Comments on Music Education," *International Musician* 60 (1962): 26.

27. "Hanson, Howard (Harold)," in *Current Biography Yearbook*, edited by Charles Moritz (New York: H. W. Wilson Company, 1966), 152–53.

28. Howard Hanson, "UNESCO and World Peace," *Educational Music Magazine* 29 (January–February 1950): 9.

29. See Howard Hanson, *Montgomery Lectures on Contemporary Civilization: Music in Contemporary American Civilization* (Lincoln: University of Nebraska, 1951).

30. See Norma Lee Browning, *Joe Maddy of Interlochen* (Chicago: Henry Regnery Company, 1963), 194, 198, 203, 219; and David Russell Williams, *Conversations with Howard Hanson*, 53.

31. Howard Hanson, "Eastman School Broadcasts of 1941–1942," *Eastman School of Music Alumni Bulletin* 13 no. 1 (1941): 10–11.

32. "Hanson Conducts, Speaks," *Rochester Democrat and Chronicle,* 20 November 1960, section F: 4; "Hanson a Hit on Coast," *Rochester Democrat and Chronicle,* 4 December 1960, section F: 4; "World Premiere of Hanson's 'The First Time' on Oct. 24 by Los Angeles Philharmonic," *Musical Leader* 95 (October 1963): 14; Allen, "At 70, Howard Hanson Looks Mostly Forward": 4.

33. John Beck, telephone conversation with the author, 25 January 2002; Robert Gauldin, telephone conversation with the author, 21 April 2002; Vincent Lenti, personal interview with the author, 29 July 2002. See also Burnet C. Tuthill, "Howard Hanson," *The Musical Quarterly* 22 (1936): 149; David Russell Williams, "Howard Hanson (1896–1981)," *Perspectives of New Music* 20 (1981): 12–25; and testimonials from Hanson's students in the last chapter of Williams's *Conversations with Howard Hanson.*

34. Howard Hanson, *Montgomery Lectures on Contemporary Civilization*, 27.

35. Hanson arranged to pay for the copying of string parts, and occasionally other duplicate parts, beginning with the third American Composers' Concert. See Kalyn, "Constructing a Nation's Music," 182–83.

36. Howard Hanson, "The Rochester Group of American Composers," in *American Composers on American Music*, edited by Henry Cowell (New York: Frederick Ungar, 1962), 85. The original edition of this book appeared in 1933.

37. Aaron Copland and Vivian Perlis, *Copland: 1900 through 1942* (New York: St. Martin's/Marek, 1984), 86.

38. Letter to the Music Editor of *The New York Times*, quoted in *Letters of Composers*, edited by Gertrude Norman and Miriam Lubell Shrifte (New York: Alfred A. Knopf, 1946), 375.

39. Olin Downes, "American Music at Rochester Festival," *New York Times*, 31 May 1931, section X: 8.

40. Madeleine Goss, *Modern Music-Makers* (New York: E. P. Dutton and Company, 1952), 231. See also Nicholas E. Tawa, *Serenading the Reluctant Eagle* (New York: Schirmer Books, 1984), 90.

41. Hanson, *Montgomery Lectures on Contemporary Civilization*, 29.

42. See, for instance, David Ewen, *American Composers: A Biographical Dictionary* (New York: G. P. Putnam's Sons, 1982), 302; Kalyn, "Constructing a Nation's Music," 306; and Nicolas Slonimsky, *Baker's Biographical Dictionary of Musicians*, 715.

43. See Kalyn, "Constructing a Nation's Music," 32, 308–9. Vincent Lenti, in a personal interview with the author (29 July 2002), expressed similar

views, and said that by the late 1950s, younger composers felt that Hanson was uninterested in performing works in the most modern style.

44. John Brzustowicz, telephone conversation with the author, 26 February 2003.

45. See also *American Composers' Concerts and Festivals of American Music 1925–1971: Cumulative Repertoire* (Rochester: The Institute of American Music of the University of Rochester, 1972), and Kalyn, "Constructing a Nation's Music," 140 (footnote 98), 191–92, 205–06, 214–15, 309, and the entirety of Appendix 14, 519–849.

46. See Kalyn, "Constructing a Nation's Music," 200.

47. John M. Conly, "American Music Played Here," *High Fidelity* 8 (February 1958): 34.

48. Alfred Frankenstein, review of Mercury MG 50165/SR 90165, *High Fidelity* 12 (March 1962): 78; Tawa, *Serenading the Reluctant Eagle*, 73.

49. During Hanson's tenure at the Eastman School, the Rochester Philharmonic's music directors were Albert Coates, Eugene Goossens, Jose Iturbi, Erich Leinsdorf, and Theodore Bloomfield.

50. Howard Hanson, "Autobiography," Chapter 36 [originally 33C], 5. This can be found in the private archive of Hanson material in the possession of John Brzustowicz.

51. The Howard Hanson Papers at the Sibley Library include notes for, or copies of, well over three hundred such talks and one hundred fifty such articles, which probably represent a small fraction of the total. (See the citation for the Howard Hanson Papers in the Bibliography. These notes and articles can be found in Boxes 1 through 13.) The Hanson archives in the possession of John Brzustowicz undoubtedly include many more.

52. Harold C. Schonberg, "Howard Hanson Is Dead; Composer and Teacher," *New York Times,* 28 February 1981: 19; Joseph Machlis, *Introduction to Contemporary Music* (New York: W. W. Norton and Company, 1951), 545; William Grant Still quoted in Goss, *Modern Music-Makers*, 212. Still's ballet *Sahdji* was dedicated to Hanson. For more on Hanson's championship of Still's music, and his support of Still with both money and influence, see William Grant Still, "Personal Notes," in Catherine Parsons Smith, *William Grant Still: A Study in Contradictions* (Berkeley: University of California Press, 2000), 232; Verna Arvey, *In One Lifetime* (Fayetteville: University of Arkansas Press, 1984), and Kalyn, "Constructing a Nation's Music," 280–94. According to John Brzustowicz, Hanson gave financial support to other American composers as well, and helped to arrange a Guggenheim grant for Harry Partch (telephone conversation with the author, 3 December 2002). For a sampling of other tributes to Hanson's efforts on behalf of American music, see Martha Alter, "American Composers, XVI: Howard Hanson," *Modern Music* 18 (1941): 84–89; William C. Hartshorn, "Music in Our Public Schools: Education and the Creative Arts" and "American Composers—Howard Hanson," *Musical Courier* 159 (April 1959): 41; Milton Cross and David Ewen, *Milton Cross' Encyclopedia of the Great Composers and Their Music* (Garden City: Doubleday and Company, Inc., 1962), 349; Ewen, *American Composers: A Biographical Dictionary*, 302–03; John Tasker Howard, *Our Contemporary Composers: American Music in the Twentieth Century* (New York: Thomas Y.

Crowell Company, 1965), 430; Slonimsky, *Baker's Biographical Dictionary of Musicians*, 715; and Tawa, *Serenading the Reluctant Eagle*, 73.

53. Quoted in Gilbert Chase, *America's Music from the Pilgrims to the Present* (New York: McGraw-Hill Book Company, Inc., 1955), 549.

54. Hanson quotes this theme in at least three of his later works: the *Elegy*, *Song of Democracy*, and *A Sea Symphony*.

55. John Brustowicz, telephone conversation with the author, 3 December 2002.

56. "Koussevitsky Lauds Hanson," *Rochester Times-Union*, 11 December 1939, section A: 3. One review of this symphony is so interesting that I cannot resist quoting from it: "Howard Hanson's Third Symphony proved once again how skillful, fine and ambitious a composer he is. It rightly won acclaim for its clear, excellent writing . . . the sombre atmosphere reminds one of Sibelius. To me this work compares more than favorably with the best works of the Finnish composer. . . . [I]t has many more interesting musical events and more meaty material." This was written by Elliott Carter. See "American Music in the New York Scene," *Modern Music* 17 (1940): 97.

57. There are references in a number of books and articles to the Symphony no. 4 having been awarded the first Pulitzer Prize in music, but they are incorrect. The first Pulitzer Prize had been awarded in the previous year to William Schuman for his Secular Cantata no. 2. Another source of confusion is that prior to 1943, fellowship awards that were called "Pulitzer Prizes" had been given for several years, including one to a doctoral student at the Eastman School.

58. There had already been at least two other American operas with the same title, by David Stanley Smith and Arthur Nevin.

59. See Irving Kolodin, *The Story of the Metropolitan Opera* (New York: Alfred A. Knopf, 1953), 441.

60. See Howard Hanson and John W. Freeman, "C Major Chord: A Dialogue with Howard Hanson," *Opera News* 28 (16 November 1963): 10–11.

61. Interview, "Music Through the Night," on WNYC-FM, 1956. A recording can be found in the Howard Hanson Papers, Box 102, tapes nos. HA21 and HA22.

62. Like Bartók and other twentieth-century composers, Hanson began to neglect the assignment of opus numbers to major works in the middle of his compositional career, and after 1964 abandoned them entirely. Although the *Elegy* is his Opus 44 and the *Bold Island Suite* of 1960 is Opus 46, *Mosaics* never received an opus number, and Hanson apparently never chose an Opus 45. It is not even clear whether Opus 45 would have been *Mosaics* or the *Song of Democracy*, another major work from the same period.

63. See Kalyn, "Constructing a Nation's Music," 152, and early reviews of Hanson's music in James E. Perone, *Howard Hanson: A Bio-Bibliography* (Westport, CT, and London: Greenwood Press, 1993), 47, 98–99.

64. Quoted in David Ewen, *American Composers: A Biographical Dictionary*, 304.

65. This issue is discussed briefly in Perone, *Howard Hanson: A Bio-Bibliography*, 8.

66. John Brzustowicz has suggested that their marriage was neither as happy nor as conventional as it appeared (telephone conversation with the author, 3 December 2002). Such details, if they are true, are beyond the scope of this book.

67. Allen, "At 70, Howard Hanson Looks Mostly Forward": 4.

68. Two of the poems in *A Sea Symphony* had already been set to music by Hanson more than sixty years earlier, in his *Three Songs from Walt Whitman*, Opus 3, for voice and orchestra. However, the music in the later work is entirely different, and shows no relationship to that of the earlier one.

69. Hanson, "Autobiography," Chapter 36 [33C], 5.

70. Michael Walsh, "Hanson donates $100,000 to Eastman," *Rochester Democrat and Chronicle,* 27 January 1976, section C: 1. According to John Brzustowicz, Hanson also gave $100,000 or its equivalent to both Northwestern University and the College of the Pacific.

71. Howard Hanson, "The New Eastman Institute of American Music," *Pan Pipes of Sigma Alpha Iota* 57 (1965): 20–21; disappointment according to John Brzustowicz, telephone conversation with the author, 16 December 2002.

72. In regard to Hanson's prominence and popularity, see for instance Tawa, *Serenading the Reluctant Eagle*, 74, and Monroe, "Howard Hanson: American Music Educator," 184. Representative samplings of critical reactions to Hanson's music can be found in Perone, *Howard Hanson: A Bio-Bibliography*, 9–105, 161–75.

73. For brief but thought-provoking discussions of this change and of the wider aesthetic and social issues involved, see Tawa, *Serenading the Reluctant Eagle*, 214–25, and the first chapter of Walter Simmons, *Voices in the Wilderness: Six American Neo-Romantic Composers* (Lanham, MD: Scarecrow Press, 2003). To contend that this change was due to the predominance in American musical life of serialism, as has often been asserted, would be simplistic; see Joseph N. Straus, "The Myth of Serial 'Tyranny' in the 1950s and 1960s," *Musical Quarterly* 83 (1999) 301–343. Nevertheless, many American musicians who lived through this period can attest to having experienced derision, intimidation, and even persecution for writing or defending tonal music. See for example Anthony Tommasini, "Midcentury Serialists: The Bullies or the Besieged?" *New York Times,* 9 July 2000, section 2: 23, and the exchange of letters in subsequent issues of the Sunday *Times*.

74. For a brief discussion of this trend and its effect on Barber's career, see Barbara Heyman, *Samuel Barber: the Composer and His Music* (New York: Oxford University Press, 1992), 427, 455–514 *passim*.

75. Quoted in Edward T. Cone, "Conversations with Aaron Copland," in *Perspectives on American Composers*, edited by Benjamin Boretz and Edward T. Cone (New York: Norton, 1971), 144. For a similar perspective, see Richard Taruskin, review of *The Harmonic Organization of "The Rite of Spring"* by Allen Forte, *Current Musicology* 28 (1978): 115. Lively, if nonscholarly, looks at similar and roughly contemporaneous trends in the fields of painting and architecture can be found in two books by Tom Wolfe, *The Painted Word* (New York: Farrar, Straus & Giroux, 1975) and *From Bauhaus to Our House* (New York: Farrar Straus Giroux, 1981).

76. Donal Henahan, "The Hanson Legacy: Challenges to Modernity in American Music," *New York Times,* 28 February 1981: 19.

77. Schonberg, "Howard Hanson Is Dead; Composer and Teacher": 19.

78. "Milestones," *Time* 117 (9 March 1981): 74.

79. See for instance *Contemporary Music Review* 6, part 2 (1992), which is entirely devoted to the subject of tonality in contemporary music. An eloquent defense of that issue of the journal, and its affirmative stance on this subject, can be found in Fred Lerdahl, "Tonality and Paranoia: A Reply to Boros," *Perspectives of New Music* 34 (1996): 242–51.

80. Tom Godell, review of works by Karl Weigl, *American Record Guide* 65 (September–October 2002): 189.

CHAPTER 3
A SUMMARY OF *HARMONIC MATERIALS OF MODERN MUSIC*

81. *Harmonic Materials* is still (theoretically) in print. Copies of the original printing were available, as recently as the turn of the twenty-first century, from Irvington Publishers in New York City. The fact that the original printing had never sold out indicates how few copies must have been sold in the four decades since its publication.

82. The reader unfamiliar with the terminology of set theory can find a concise summary in the first three chapters of Joseph N. Straus's textbook *Introduction to Post-Tonal Theory* (Englewood Cliffs: Prentice-Hall, 2000). An extremely brief but useful summary can also be found on pages 3–24 of Janet Schmalfeldt's *Berg's "Wozzeck": Harmonic Language and Dramatic Design* (New Haven: Yale University Press, 1983).

83. The bracketed term shows the prime form, or the most compact ordering of the set class, transposed to begin on zero (with 0 representing the pitch class C, 1 representing D♭, and so on). The interval vector shows the number of occurrences of each interval class among the elements of a set, listed in order from ic 1 to ic 6. So the interval vector 210000 shows that the set class with prime form C-D♭-D has two occurrences of interval class 1 (that is, of one semitone), one occurrence of interval class 2, and no occurrences of interval classes 3, 4, 5 or 6.

84. As an example for the benefit of readers unfamiliar with set theory, the five-tone sonority C-C♯-D-E-G (called $p^2s^2d^2$ in Hanson's system, and set class 5-Z36 [01247] in set theory) contains, between pairs of its members, two perfect fifths (or fourths), one major third (or minor sixth), two minor thirds (or major sixths), two major seconds (or minor sevenths), two minor seconds (or major sevenths) and one tritone; the five-tone sonority C-C♯-D♯-F-F♯ (n^2s^2t in Hanson's system and sc 5-Z12 [01356] in set theory) contains exactly the same numbers of each interval class. However, no combination of transposition and inversion can transform one of these sonorities into the other. Thus, although they are not equivalent in terms of transposition or inversion, they have a unique relationship which Hanson calls isomeric and set theorists call the Z-relation.

85. David Russell Williams, *Conversations with Howard Hanson* (Arkadelphia, Ark.: Delta Publications, 1988), 42.

86. Although Hanson does not identify it as such, this is in fact the same method of adding "foreign tones" to extend the projection that he used in previous projections. For example, adding a tritone to each of the first three tones of the perfect-fifth projection C-G-D produces C-F♯-G-C♯-D-G♯, which is exactly what would be produced by taking the simple tritone projection C-F♯, then adding the "foreign tone" G and its tritone C♯, then adding the next foreign tone D and its tritone G♯.

87. *Berg's "Wozzeck,"* 246.

88. Hanson's sonority names on the master diagram and in his last chapter contain a number of errors or inconsistencies. These will be discussed in later chapters of this book, where relevant.

CHAPTER 4
THE THEORY CONSIDERED AS A SYSTEM

89. The reader unfamiliar with the concepts and terminology of set theory can refer to one of the standard texts, such as Joseph N. Straus's *Introduction to Post-Tonal Theory* (Upper Saddle River, NJ: Prentice Hall, 2000) and John Rahn's *Basic Atonal Theory* (New York and London: Longman, 1980), or to the brief summary on pages 3–24 of Janet Schmalfeldt, *Berg's "Wozzeck": Harmonic Language and Dramatic Design* (New Haven: Yale University Press, 1983).

90. For much of the information in the following paragraphs I am indebted to Jonathan W. Bernard's article "Chord, Collection, and Set in Twentieth-Century Theory," in *Music Theory in Concept and Practice*, edited by James M. Baker, David W. Beach, and Jonathan W. Bernard (Rochester: University of Rochester Press, 1997), 11–51; and to Allen Forte's article on "Theory" in *Dictionary of Contemporary Music*, edited by John Vinton (New York: E. P. Dutton & Co., 1974), 753–61.

91. H. J. Vincent, *Ist unsere Harmonielehre wirklich eine Theorie?* (Vienna: Rörich, n.d.). See also Robert W. Wason, "Progressive Harmonic Theory in the Mid-Nineteenth Century," *Journal of Musicological Research* 8 (1988): 55–90.

92. Ernst Bacon, "Our Musical Idiom," *The Monist* 27 (1917): 560–607.

93. Josef Matthias Hauer, "Sphärenmusik," *Melos* 3 (1922): 132–33. See also George Perle, "The Possible Chords in Twelve-Tone Music," *The Score and I.M.A. Magazine* 9 (1954): 54–58; Roberto Gerhard, "Reply to George Perle," *The Score and I.M.A. Magazine* 9 (1954): 59–60; and Richmond Browne, review of *The Structure of Atonal Music* by Allen Forte, *Journal of Music Theory* 18 (1974): 412–14.

94. Fritz Heinrich Klein, "Die Grenze der Halbtonwelt," *Die Musik* 17 (1925): 281–86; for a translation and discussion, see Dave Headlam, "Fritz Heinrich Klein's 'Die Grenze der Halbtonwelt' and *Die Maschine*," *Theoria* 6 (1992): 79–96. Alois Hába, *Neue Harmonielehre des diatonischen, chromatischen, Viertel-, Drittel-, Sechstel-, und Zwölftel-Tonsystems* (Leipzig: Kistner & Siegel, 1927); for a commentary on Hába's errors, and a correct calculation of the number of distinct pc sets that was apparently independent of Klein's, see Perle, "The Possible Chords in Twelve-Tone Music," and also Bernard,

"Chord, Collection, and Set in Twentieth-Century Theory": 28–30. It should also be noted that several minor aspects of both Hanson's theory and set theory were anticipated by Paul Hindemith in *Unterweisung im Tonsatz* (1937), published in English as *The Craft of Musical Composition*, tr. Arthur Mendel (New York: B. Schott's Söhne, 1942); by Joseph Schillinger in *The Schillinger System of Musical Composition* (New York: Carl Fischer, Inc., 1946, in two volumes); and by Nicolas Slonimsky in *Thesaurus of Scales and Melodic Patterns* (New York: Charles Scribner's Sons, 1947); a summary of these anticipations can be found in Bernard, "Chord, Collection, and Set in Twentieth-Century Theory." In addition, Pierre Boulez used procedures somewhat similar to projection in the "multiplication" he performed on segments of a twelve-tone row to compose parts of his piece *Le Marteau sans maître* (1955), although he did not discuss this practice in print until nine years later, when he mentioned it briefly in Pierre Boulez, *Penser la musique aujourd'hui* (Geneva: Editions Gonthier, 1964), published in English as *Boulez on Music Today*, translated by Susan Bradshaw and Richard Rodney Bennett (Cambridge, Mass.: Harvard University Press, 1971).

95. Milton Babbitt, "The Function of Set Structure in the Twelve-Tone System" (Ph.D. diss., Princeton University, 1946).

96. Milton Babbitt, "Some Aspects of Twelve-Tone Composition," *The Score and I.M.A. Magazine* 12 (1955): 53–61; "Twelve-Tone Invariants as Compositional Determinants," *Musical Quarterly* 46 (1960): 246–59; "Set Structure as a Compositional Determinant," *Journal of Music Theory* 5 (1961): 72–94.

97. David Lewin, "Re: Intervallic Relations Between Two Collections of Notes," *Journal of Music Theory* 3 (1959): 298–301.

98. David Russell Williams, recorded interviews of Howard Hanson (summer 1978), accession no. 000.35, Eastman School of Music Archives, Sibley Music Library, Eastman School of Music, University of Rochester, Rochester, NY. This passage is transcribed with certain differences in David Russell Williams, *Conversations with Howard Hanson* (Arkadelphia, Ark.: Delta Publications, 1988), 40.

99. John Brzustowicz, who grew up next door to Hanson in Rochester and became very close to him, believes that Hanson began work on the theory at Northwestern (telephone conversation with the author, 3 December 2002).

100. Williams, interviews of Howard Hanson. These passages are transcribed with some differences in Williams, *Conversations with Howard Hanson*, 7 and 39.

101. Howard Hanson, "The Materials of Music," Louis C. Elson Memorial Lecture presented at Harvard University, 17 and 18 March, 1948, text in Howard Hanson Papers, Box 6, Folder 9 (see the citation for the Howard Hanson Papers in the Bibliography); "Hanson Book Published; 30-Year Opus," *Rochester Times-Union*, 1 March 1960: 28; Howard Hanson, "Autobiography," Chapter 36 [originally 33C], 1 (in the private archive of Hanson material in the possession of John Brzustowicz).

102. See the letters from Emma Lou Diemer, Grant Fletcher, Roger Hannay, Richard Johnston, and Eugene J. Ulrich quoted in Williams, *Conver-*

sations with Howard Hanson, 88–99; and Robert Sutton, "Howard Hanson, Set Theory Pioneer," *Sonus* 8 (fall 1987): 17.

103. "Hanson Announces New Musical Theory," *Musical America* 71 (15 December 1951): 23.

104. "Philly Bow of Hanson Work Set," *Rochester Democrat and Chronicle*, 15 January 1955; Sutton, "Howard Hanson, Set Theory Pioneer": 18. Ruth T. Watanabe, who was close to Hanson during the later Eastman years, feels that the book may have taken so long to publish because Hanson was extremely busy and felt no particular need to rush it into print. (Telephone conversation with the author, 15 May 2002.)

105. David Lewin, "Re: The Intervallic Content of a Collection of Notes, Intervallic Relations between a Collection of Notes and Its Complement: An Application to Schoenberg's Hexachordal Pieces," *Journal of Music Theory* 4 (1960): 98–101.

106. Allen Forte, "A Theory of Set-Complexes for Music," *Journal of Music Theory* 8 (1964): 136–83.

107. Allen Forte, *The Structure of Atonal Music* (New Haven: Yale University Press, 1973).

108. To be more precise, Hanson did write about chromatic relations from a mathematical perspective, but it was a geometric one, rather than number- or group-oriented. This is clear from his many geometric diagrams in *Harmonic Materials,* and a short explanatory passage in his unpublished autobiography, Chapter 36 [33C], 2.

109. Hanson's achievement is acknowledged, albeit somewhat condescendingly and disparagingly, in Bernard, "Chord, Collection, and Set in Twentieth-Century Theory," 45–49, and Schmalfeldt, *Berg's "Wozzeck,"* 9–13. The general failure of set theorists to acknowledge Hanson's priority will be discussed later in this chapter.

110. See for instance Edward T. Cone, "Beyond Analysis," *Perspectives of New Music* 6 (1967): 33–51; William E. Benjamin, review of *The Structure of Atonal Music* by Allen Forte, *Perspectives of New Music* 13 (1973): 170–90; Eric Regener, "On Allen Forte's Theory of Chords," *Perspectives of New Music* 13 (1973): 191–211; Richmond Browne, review of *The Structure of Atonal Music* by Allen Forte: 390–415; Richard Taruskin, review of *The Harmonic Organization of "The Rite of Spring"* by Allen Forte, *Current Musicology* 28 (1978): 114–29; George Perle, "Pitch-Class Set Analysis: An Evaluation," *Journal of Musicology* 8 (1990): 151–72, and *The Listening Composer* (Berkeley: University of California Press, 1990), 30–54, 111–12. See also the reviews of *Harmonic Materials* by Boatwright and Mitchell in the Bibliography. Browne's review in particular raises cogent questions about the validity of some of the assumptions, both phenomenological and analytical, that are inherent in the concepts of pitch class, set class, and interval class—and thus in Hanson's concepts as well.

111. See, for example, Richard Taruskin's objections to Forte's use of set theory to analyze passages from Stravinsky's *The Rite of Spring*—passages that, as Taruskin argues convincingly, contain harmonies or voice-leading with origins in traditional tonal practice—in Taruskin, review of *The Harmon-*

ic Organization of "The Rite of Spring" by Allen Forte; and George Perle's analogous objections to Forte's analysis of Charles Ives's *The Unanswered Question*, in "Pitch-Class Set Analysis: An Evaluation": 160–62.

112. "This is not to imply that the interval and its inversion are the same, but rather that they perform the same function in a sonority." (*Harmonic Materials*, 9.)

113. *Harmonic Materials*, 55.

114. Williams, interviews of Howard Hanson. These passages are transcribed with some differences in Williams, *Conversations with Howard Hanson*, 43.

115. According to John Brzustowicz, Hanson became aware of a "fundamental error" in his theory just as *Harmonic Materials* was going to print. After "many years of work," he was able to correct the error, but did not publish his new work because he had "left enough material behind on the subject" for future theorists, and did not wish to devote more of his own time to publication. Brzustowicz does not know if this "error" was related to the questions raised here. (Telephone conversation with the author, 3 December 2002; letter to the author, 16 January 2003.) Hanson also mentioned in the interviews with David Russell Williams that he was "not satisfied" with the way he had presented the theory of complementary relationships.

116. *Harmonic Materials*, 4.

117. Ibid., 106–08.

118. Ibid., 4, 10.

119. Some of these problems are discussed in William J. Mitchell, review of *Harmonic Materials of Modern Music* by Howard Hanson, *Journal of Music Theory* 4 (1960): 236–43. Difficulties that these assumptions pose for analysis will be discussed further in the fifth chapter of this book.

120. The reader who has counted these lists of hexads will note that together they add up to forty-nine. Hanson knew that there are fifty hexads, of course, and if he had tallied up his groups, he might have found the error pointed out by Brian Ellard, which is described one paragraph later in the text.

121. See Brian Ellard, "Edmond Costere's *Lois et Styles des Harmonies Musicales*" (Ph.D. diss., Eastman School of Music, 1973), 133.

122. This omission was first referred to, albeit obliquely, in Godfrey Winham, review of *Harmonic Materials of Modern Music* by Howard Hanson, *Perspectives of New Music* 1 (1963): 146–47.

123. *Harmonic Materials*, 17. The italics, as in all quotations in this book from *Harmonic Materials*, are Hanson's.

124. Ibid., 18.

125. Ibid., x.

126. Ibid., 28.

127. Ibid., 233. See the summary of Chapter 35 of *Harmonic Materials* in the previous chapter of this book.

128. Ibid., 263.

129. Ibid., 325, 345.

130. Ibid., 367–68 and master diagram.

131. See also the discussion of these terms in the footnotes to Tables 6.1 and 6.2 in the sixth chapter of this book.

132. I use the qualification "relatively" because a number of theorists have found deficiencies in the terminology, definitions, and proofs of set theory, as well as in their relevance to musical events. See for instance Edward T. Cone, "A Budding Grove," *Perspectives of New Music* 3 (1965): 38–46, and Eric Regener, "On Allen Forte's Theory of Chords": 198–99.

133. Richard Chrisman makes use of this procedure, without crediting Hanson, in what he calls "successive-interval arrays," and gives a method of finding the interval succession for complementary sets, in his article "Identification and Correlation of Pitch-Sets," *Journal of Music Theory* 15 (1971): 58–83. There is a somewhat similar but more awkward procedure, also in a set-theory context, in the appendix of George Perle's *Serial Composition and Atonality* (Berkeley: University of California Press, 1991). Eric Regener, in discussing *The Structure of Atonal Music*, proposes an alternative set nomenclature (which he calls "interval notation") in which each set is represented by its interval succession, also without reference to *Harmonic Materials*. See Regener, "On Allen Forte's Theory of Chords."

134. Schmalfeldt points out that Hanson includes the all-interval tetrachords in his chapter on the projection of the minor third, although they contain no more minor thirds than any other interval. (See Schmalfeldt, *Berg's "Wozzeck,"* 247, note 22.) This is true, and at first glance it may seem incongruous; but to ascribe this to "Hanson's bias" in favor of tonality, as Schmalfeldt does, is unfair and inaccurate. Like the other sonorities described in Hanson's Chapter 12, they are subsets of the six-tone minor-third projection, and he ascribes to them no special relationship with minor thirds beyond that. In fact, as the master diagram at the back of the book shows, Hanson puts them in the category of tetrads with no predominant interval, which seems perfectly appropriate. A similar viewpoint is expressed by Ian Quinn, "Listening to Similarity Relations," *Perspectives of New Music* 39 (2001): 149.

135. See for instance Straus, 84.

136. Forte, *The Structure of Atonal Music*, 77. According to Milton Babbitt, this rule was expressed and proved first by the mathematician Ralph Fox. See Babbitt, *Words About Music*, edited by Stephen Dembski and Joseph N. Straus (Madison: University of Wisconsin Press, 1987), 104–06. David Lewin also produced an elegant version of this rule, although in relation to intervals rather than interval classes, in "Re: The Intervallic Content of a Collection of Notes, Intervallic Relations between a Collection of Notes and Its Complement: An Application to Schoenberg's Hexachordal Pieces": 99.

137. See Forte, "A Theory of Set-Complexes for Music," and *The Structure of Atonal Music*, Part 2. Few other theorists have cared to follow Forte's work in this area, despite his prominence in the field and his belief that the set complex "provides a comprehensive model of relations among pc sets in general and establishes a framework for the description, interpretation, and ex-

planation of any atonal composition" (*The Structure of Atonal Music*, 93). A prominent exception is Janet Schmalfeldt's *Berg's "Wozzeck,"* which relies heavily on Forte's set-complex theory in its concluding chapter.

138. See Forte, "A Theory of Set-Complexes for Music": 169. For a similar opinion of the superiority of the earlier format, see Browne, review of *The Structure of Atonal Music*: 406.

139. *Harmonic Materials*, 78.

140. Forte, *The Structure of Atonal Music*, 200–08.

141. Janet Schmalfeldt implicitly acknowledges this relationship when she refers to 6-35 as "the whole-tone hexachord" and the others as "the three 'almost whole-tone' hexachords." See Schmalfeldt, *Berg's "Wozzeck,"* 227.

142. See John Rahn, "Relating Sets," *Perspectives of New Music* 18 (1979–80): 483–98; David Lewin, "A Response to a Response: On PCSet Relatedness," *Perspectives of New Music* 18 (1979–80): 498–502; Marcus Castrén, *RECREL: A Similarity Measure for Set-Classes* (Helsinki: Sibelius Academy, 1994); and Ian Quinn, "Listening to Similarity Relations," *Perspectives of New Music* 39 (2001): 108–158. Quinn's article makes imaginative use of Hanson projections to reveal the similarities among different similarity measures.

143. For the expression of similar views by set theorists, see for instance John Clough, "Pitch-Set Equivalence and Inclusion (A Comment on Forte's Theory of Set-Complexes)," *Journal of Music Theory* 9 (1965): 163–71; Regener, "On Allen Forte's Theory of Chords": 205; and Quinn, "Listening to Similarity Relations": 109.

144. *Harmonic Materials,* vii–viii.

145. Procedures similar to Hanson's projections, although perhaps influenced as much by Pierre Boulez's "multiplication," have been used by Richard Cohn in his article "Inversional Symmetry and Transpositional Combination in Bartók," *Music Theory Spectrum* 10 (1988): 19–42, and by Robert Morris in "Compositional Spaces and Other Territories," *Perspectives of New Music* 33 (1995): 328–358. A more recent formulation with even closer parallels to Hanson can be found in Stephen Heinemann, "Pitch-Class Set Multiplication in Theory and Practice," *Music Theory Spectrum* 20 (1998): 72–96, although Heinemann claims closer kinship to the "interpolation," "infrapolation," and "ultrapolation" found in Nicolas Slonimsky's *Thesaurus of Scales and Melodic Patterns*. In addition, George Perle has done extensive work with interval cycles, which are essentially projections of simple intervals, in "Berg's Master Array of the Interval Cycles," *Musical Quarterly* 63 (1977): 1–30; throughout *Twelve-Tone Tonality* (Berkeley, Los Angeles, Oxford: University of California Press, 1977); and in the appendix to *Serial Composition and Atonality* (Berkeley, Los Angeles, Oxford: University of California Press, 1991). Other literature on interval cycles includes Daniel Starr and Robert Morris, "A General Theory of Combinatoriality and the Aggregate," *Perspectives of New Music* 16/1 (1977): 3–35, 16/2 (1978) 50–84; Elliott Antokoletz, "Interval Cycles in Stravinsky's Early Ballets," *Journal of the*

American Musicological Society 34 (1986): 578–614; Richard Cohn, "Properties and Generability of Transpositionally Invariant Sets," *Journal of Music Theory* 35 (1991): 1–32; and Ian Quinn, "Listening to Similarity Relations." Of these, only Cohn and Quinn have followed Hanson in going beyond the study of simple interval cycles to incorporate the projections of larger and more complex sonorities, and Quinn seems to be the only set theorist who has acknowledged in print not only Hanson's priority in the study of interval cycles, but the fecundity of his concepts and techniques for further exploration.

146. Nicolas Slonimsky, review of *Harmonic Materials of Modern Music* by Howard Hanson, *Notes* 18 (1961): 415–16. See also the entries under Boatwright, George, Lloyd, Mitchell, Werlé, and Winham in the Bibliography.

147. Williams, interviews of Howard Hanson. This passage is transcribed with some differences in Williams, *Conversations with Howard Hanson*, 41.

148. Bernard, "Chord, Collection, and Set in Twentieth-Century Theory," 47–48.

149. Howard Hanson, "Autobiography," Chapter 36 [33C], 1.

150. Forte, "A Theory of Set-Complexes for Music": 180–81, note 11.

151. Forte, "A Theory of Set-Complexes for Music": 143; Clough, "Pitch-Set Equivalence and Inclusion (A Comment on Forte's Theory of Set-Complexes)"; Allen Forte, "The Domain and Relations of Set-Complex Theory," *Journal of Music Theory* 9 (1965): 173–80; Forte, *The Structure of Atonal Music*, 5. Forte's article on "Theory" in *Dictionary of Contemporary Music*, 753–61, also lists *Harmonic Materials* in its bibliography, but makes no mention of Hanson in the text.

152. Lewin, "Re: The Intervallic Content of a Collection of Notes, Intervallic Relations between a Collection of Notes and Its Complement: An Application to Schoenberg's Hexachordal Pieces." See Forte, "A Theory of Set-Complexes for Music": 180, note 10, and *The Structure of Atonal Music*, 21, note.

153. Discussion of sc 5-Z12 in Forte, *The Structure of Atonal Music*, 45, note; discussion of interval vectors of complements in Forte, "A Theory of Set-Complexes for Music": 182, note 15, and *The Structure of Atonal Music*, 77. See *Harmonic Materials*, 331–34, 351–52.

154. In fact, the journal that published Lewin's article carried a review of *Harmonic Materials* in the next issue. See William J. Mitchell, review of *Harmonic Materials of Modern Music* by Howard Hanson.

155. Perle, "Pitch-Class Set Analysis: An Evaluation": 163; Schmalfeldt, *Berg's "Wozzeck,"* 10. Strangely, Jonathan W. Bernard credits Lewin with being the first to discuss the concept of the Z-relation in print in 1960, even though one page later he acknowledges that Hanson discusses Z-related sets (as "isomers") in *Harmonic Materials*. Giving the priority to Lewin may have been an inadvertent slip on Bernard's part due to his having discussed Lewin first, because Lewin's earlier article (which does not mention the Z-relation concept) appeared in 1959. Possibly also Bernard did not wish to contradict

Forte in a book intended as a *Festschrift* for him—a book that, in a further irony, was published by the Eastman School of Music. See Bernard, "Chord, Collection, and Set in Twentieth-Century Theory," 45–46.

156. Schmalfeldt, *Berg's "Wozzeck,"* 13, 16. This is especially strange in that it contradicts Schmalfeldt's earlier, if qualified, acknowledgment of Hanson's priority in identifying and describing the Z-relation, as mentioned in the previous paragraph.

157. Schmalfeldt, *Berg's "Wozzeck,"* 10. See also Bernard, "Chord, Collection, and Set in Twentieth-Century Theory," 48–49. On the other hand, Schmalfeldt's and Bernard's criticisms of the unsystematic nature of Hanson's derivations for different projections, which Schmalfeldt calls "the most problematic aspect" of the book, seem quite valid.

158. Forte, "A Theory of Set-Complexes for Music": 182, note 14.

159. Articles with such citations include Richard Cohn's "Inversional Symmetry and Transpositional Combination in Bartók," Robert Morris's "Compositional Spaces and Other Territories," and Stephen Heinemann's "Pitch-Class Set Multiplication in Theory and Practice." In addition to the works by Perle, Schmalfeldt, Bernard and Quinn already discussed, and the reviews of *Harmonic Materials* already mentioned, see also the entries under Jackson, Moomaw, and Parker in the Bibliography.

160. For much of the information in this and the following paragraphs, I am indebted to the Eastman School of Music alumni office; to the Department of Music and Dance office at the University of Massachusetts at Amherst; to Robert Sutton, "Howard Hanson, Set Theory Pioneer": 17–18; to telephone conversations with present and former Eastman faculty members Robert Morris (19 November 2001), Vincent Lenti (21 January 2002), John Beck (25 January 2002), William Francis McBeth (25 January 2002 and 18 March 2003), David Russell Williams (25 January 2002), Robert Gauldin (21 April 2002), and Ruth T. Watanabe (15 May 2002); and to a telephone conversation with Sutton's widow, Mary Lynn Carroll (13 April 2003).

161. See the letters from Emma Lou Diemer, Grant Fletcher, Roger Hannay, Richard Johnston, and Eugene J. Ulrich quoted in Williams, *Conversations with Howard Hanson*, 88–99.

162. Robert Sutton, "Howard Hanson, Set Theory Pioneer."

163. Mary Lynn Carroll, telephone conversation with the author, 13 April 2003. Carroll, who had studied the Hanson theory under Sutton at the University of Massachusetts, and was married to Sutton for many years, says that he never said anything to indicate that he had made more than a small contribution to the book or the theory. She believes that he might have helped with the editing.

164. There are hundreds or thousands of such pages scattered throughout many files in the Howard Hanson Papers in the Sibley Music Library. John Brzustowicz also has an uncounted number of them in his private archive, several hundred of which I have seen in photocopy. Brzustowicz claims to have many papers of Hanson's containing theoretical work on the chromatic scale, dating from as far back as Hanson's days at the College of the Pacific (1916–1921).

165. This will be discussed further, in connection with Hanson's Symphony no. 3, in the last chapter of this book.

166. The sketches for the Piano Concerto can be found in the Howard Hanson Papers, Box 34, Folders 6 and 7. See the citation for the Howard Hanson Papers in the Bibliography.

167. These pages can be found in the Howard Hanson Papers, Box 62, Folder 4.

CHAPTER 5
THE THEORY CONSIDERED AS A METHOD OF ANALYSIS

168. *Harmonic Materials*, 120. All musical examples in this chapter duplicate the excerpts as they appear in *Harmonic Materials*, except that Example 5.1 omits the last three measures of the *Symphony of Psalms* excerpt as quoted by Hanson.

169. See, for example, Pieter van den Toorn, *The Music of Igor Stravinsky* (New Haven: Yale University Press, 1983), 344–51.

170. See the summaries of Chapters 11 and 13 of *Harmonic Materials* in the third chapter of this book. The name C. N^3 denotes the complement of N^3, the minor-third tetrad. (The octad could also be called N^7.) As explained in the fourth chapter of this book, the capitalized interval symbol signifies a reflexive projection—in this case, an interval projected upon itself the number of times shown in the superscript. The prefix "C." before a sonority name denotes the complement of that sonority; Hanson uses it in the names of all sonorities with eight or more elements, and some of the seven-tone sonorities as well.

171. See the summaries of Chapters 11 and 12 of *Harmonic Materials* in the third chapter of this book.

172. Igor Stravinsky and Robert Craft, *Dialogues and a Diary* (London: Faber and Faber, 1968), 45.

173. See the summary of Chapter 19 of *Harmonic Materials* in the third chapter of this book.

174. *Harmonic Materials,* 155–56.

175. The excerpts mentioned are from Igor Stravinsky, *Petrushka*, Second Tableau: rapidly alternating or simultaneous F♯ major and C major triads (*Harmonic Materials*, 155); Benjamin Britten, *Les Illuminations,* "Fanfare": alternating E major and B♭ major triads (*Harmonic Materials*, 155); Claude Debussy, *Pelleas et Mélisande*, Act II, Scene 3: alternating C major and D♯ minor triads (*Harmonic Materials,* 203); Ottorino Respighi, *Pini di Roma*, "I pini di Villa Borghese": alternating A, F♯ and D major triads in trumpet fanfare (*Harmonic Materials*, 171); and Gustav Holst, *The Hymn of Jesus*, "Divine Grace is dancing," alternating E major and B♭ minor triads (*Harmonic Materials,* 199). The Holst analysis is criticized on similar grounds in William J. Mitchell, review of *Harmonic Materials of Modern Music* by Howard Hanson, *Journal of Music Theory* 4 (1960): 239.

176. *Harmonic Materials*, 171.

177. See the summary of Chapter 22 of *Harmonic Materials* in the third chapter of this book.

178. Some of these problems are pointed out in Howard Boatwright, review of *Harmonic Materials of Modern Music* by Howard Hanson, *Journal of the American Musicological Society* 17 (1964): 412–13. Analogous problems have been found in analyses using set theory, even in analyses of nontonal music. William E. Benjamin makes several cogent objections to Forte's analyses and adds, "I am not denying the importance of set structure. I am merely trying to show that pitch structure is not adequately explained in terms of set structure." See William E. Benjamin, review of *The Structure of Atonal Music* by Allen Forte, *Perspectives of New Music* 13 (1973): 170–90.

179. *Harmonic Materials*, 198. (Hanson has erroneously omitted the dot after the G# eighth-note. As always in *Harmonic Materials,* he spells Stravinsky's title as *Petrouchka*.)

180. Ibid., 88.

181. Objections have been made to what appear to be similarly arbitrary choices in set-theory analysis. See for instance Richard Taruskin, review of *The Harmonic Organization of "The Rite of Spring"* by Allen Forte, *Current Musicology* 28 (1978): 122.

182. Such a reaction can be found in Godfrey Winham, review of *Harmonic Materials of Modern Music* by Howard Hanson, *Perspectives of New Music* 1 (1963): 146–47.

183. For a brief discussion of these issues, see Joseph N. Straus, *Introduction to Post-Tonal Theory* (Upper Saddle River, NJ: Prentice Hall, 2000), 51–52.

184. *Harmonic Materials*, 270–2. When a musical work, or a section thereof, is described in this or subsequent chapters as being "in C" without a mode appended or "C-centric," it will be understood to mean that the piece or section has C as a tonal center, in a manner common to many tonally-centric works of the twentieth century, without being in any one particular or traditional mode. For example, the first movement of Bartók's Concerto for Orchestra (after the introductory section) can be said with some degree of validity to be "in F," although his use of quartal structures both melodically and harmonically, as well as the presence of G♭ instead of G at the final cadence, would preclude the use of "F minor" as inaccurate.

185. Again, similar criticisms have been made of set-theory analysis. See for example Taruskin, review of *The Harmonic Organization of "The Rite of Spring"*: 128.

186. Harmonic Materials, viii.

CHAPTER 6
THE TWO DEMONSTRATION PIECES

187. David Russell Williams, *Conversations with Howard Hanson* (Arkadelphia, Ark.: Delta Publications, 1988), 7.

188. The notes can be found as the Foreword to the published score, and also as the liner notes and as part of the oral analysis on the long-playing vinyl recording *The Composer and His Orchestra Vol. III: An Analysis, with*

Musical Illustrations, of Howard Hanson's "For the First Time," Eastman Philharmonia, cond. Howard Hanson (Mercury Records MG50357 & SR90357, 1963). A small part of the original liner notes—without any of the technical discussions—appears in the booklet of a double-compact-disc reissue, *The Composer and His Orchestra* (Mercury 434 370–2, 1996), which includes the oral analysis.

189. See James E. Perone, *Howard Hanson: a Bio-Bibliography* (Westport, CT, and London: Greenwood Press, 1993), 85, 104; and also Marilyn V. Plain, *Howard Hanson: A Comprehensive Catalog of the Manuscripts* (Rochester: Eastman School of Music Press, 1997), 34–37.

190. See the citation for the Howard Hanson Papers in the Bibliography. The sketches associated with *For the First Time* are in Box 38, Folder 4. *For the First Time* is dedicated, not to Alberta Hartshorn, but to Claudette Sorel.

191. See Volume 1 ("For Beginners") of *The New Scribner Music Library* (New York: Charles Scribner's Sons, 1964), 86–87.

192. See the citation for the Howard Hanson Papers in the Bibliography. The materials associated with *Young Person's Guide* are in Box 58, Folders 5 through 11, and Box 59, Folder 1. This piece is listed as *Young People's Guide to the Six-tone Scale* in James E. Perone, *Howard Hanson: A Bio-Bibliography* (Westport, CT, and London: Greenwood Press, 1993), 93ff.

193. From the Foreword to the printed score, also printed as the liner notes to the long-playing vinyl recording *Young Composer's Guide to the Six Tone Scale,* Eastman Wind Ensemble, cond. Donald Hunsberger (Mercury Golden Imports SRI 75132, 1978).

194. David Russell Williams, recorded interviews of Howard Hanson (summer 1978), accession no. 000.35, Eastman School of Music Archives, Sibley Music Library, Eastman School of Music, University of Rochester, Rochester, NY. This passage is transcribed with certain differences in Williams, *Conversations with Howard Hanson*, 7–8. Williams mentions this aspect of Hanson's personality on a number of occasions during the interviews.

195. *Harmonic Materials*, 370.

CHAPTER 7
THE INFLUENCE OF THE THEORY ON HANSON'S LATER COMPOSITIONS

196. David Russell Williams, recorded interviews of Howard Hanson (summer 1978), accession no. 000.35, Eastman School of Music Archives, Sibley Music Library, Eastman School of Music, University of Rochester, Rochester, NY. This passage is transcribed in two different places, with various differences, in David Russell Williams, *Conversations with Howard Hanson* (Arkadelphia, Ark.: Delta Publications, 1988), 7, 40.

197. Williams, *Conversations with Howard Hanson,* 1, 6.

198. Several of these pieces have previously been analyzed—*Sinfonia Sacra* and Symphony no. 6 in Alan Philip Witucki, "Thematic Transformation and Other Considerations in the Six Symphonies of Howard Hanson" (Mas-

ter's thesis, Michigan State University, 1978), and *Mosaics* and Symphony no. 6 in Mark Mason Parker, "Classification of Pitch Materials in Three Compositions by Howard Hanson" (Master's thesis, Eastman School of Music, 1976). In this book, however, I have used my own analyses.

199. Quoted by Steven C. Smith in the liner notes to the recording of *Sinfonia Sacra* by the Seattle Symphony under Gerard Schwarz on Delos compact disc D100111 (1992). In a radio interview about two years after he wrote it, Hanson said that it was inspired by the story of Mary Magdalene at the tomb of Christ on the first Easter. (Unidentified interview on WFMT, Chicago, approximately 1957. A recording can be found in the Howard Hanson Papers, Box 102, tapes nos. HA8 and HA9.)

200. Williams, *Conversations with Howard Hanson,* 17–18.

201. Ibid., 6.

202. This technique of alteration or "modulation" of sonorities will be discussed shortly in relation to Hanson's *Elegy*.

203. See the citation for the Howard Hanson Papers in the Bibliography. The sketches associated with the *Elegy* can be found in Box 38, Folder 12.

204. In regard to this technique, see the summaries of Chapters 4 and 7 of *Harmonic Materials* in the third chapter of this book.

205. This piece is usually, and erroneously, called *Nymphs and Satyr,* not only on its recordings but even in James E. Perone's generally authoritative *Howard Hanson: A Bio-Bibliography* (Westport, CT, and London: Greenwood Press, 1993), 19ff.

206. Williams, interviews of Howard Hanson. This passage is transcribed with some differences in Williams, *Conversations with Howard Hanson,* 1.

207. Williams, interviews of Howard Hanson. This passage is transcribed with some differences in Williams, *Conversations with Howard Hanson,* 6.

208. *Harmonic Materials*, 173.

209. See Appendix H, line 9.

210. Williams, interviews of Howard Hanson. This passage does not appear in *Conversations with Howard Hanson*, but its context can be found on page 7. According to Mark Mason Parker, in a personal interview on 11 March 1975 Hanson said that *Mosaics* "is one of the works in which the influence of his pitch classification methods on his compositional procedures is most vividly illustrated." See Parker, "Classification of Pitch Materials in Three Compositions by Howard Hanson," xiv.

211. See the citation for the Howard Hanson Papers in the Bibliography. The material associated with *Mosaics* can be found in Box 43, Folders 1 and 2, and Box 64, Folder 8.

212. Quoted in liner notes for *Mosaics*, Eastman-Rochester Orchestra, cond. Howard Hanson (Mercury Records MG50430 and SR90430, 1965).

213. Williams, interviews of Howard Hanson. This passage is transcribed with some differences in Williams, *Conversations with Howard Hanson,* 1–2.

214. Williams, *Conversations with Howard Hanson*, 2.

215. See the citation for the Howard Hanson Papers in the Bibliography. The material associated with the Piano Concerto can be found in Box 34, Folders 6 and 7.

216. See the summaries of Chapters 34 and 35 of *Harmonic Materials* in the third chapter of this book.

217. As mentioned in the fourth chapter of this book, according to his friend and neighbor John Brzustowicz, Hanson became aware of a "fundamental error" in his theory just as *Harmonic Materials* was going to print, and later corrected the error, although he never published his revisions. (Telephone conversation with the author, 3 December 2002; letter to the author, 16 January 2003.)

218. See the citation for the Howard Hanson Papers in the Bibliography. This notebook can be found in Box 86, Folder 6.

219. See the citation for the Howard Hanson Papers in the Bibliography. Such notebooks can be found in a number of locations throughout the Papers; these particular notebooks can be found in Box 113, Folders 2 and 5.

220. *Harmonic Materials*, xi.

221. See the reviews quoted in James E. Perone, *Howard Hanson: A Bio-Bibliography*, 173–75.

222. The first, and as of this writing the only, commercial recording of the piano version of *For the First Time* can be found on *Howard Hanson: Piano Music*, Thomas Labé, piano (Naxos compact disc 8.559047, 2000). This was a first recording for most of Hanson's piano pieces, but all of them except *For the First Time* and one other were very early pieces, written before Hanson's time in Rome.

223. According to the late Arthur Cohn of Carl Fischer, Inc., Hanson's publisher for many years, these two pieces have had far fewer performances than Hanson's other mature orchestral works. (Personal communication with the author, November 1995.)

224. Williams, *Conversations with Howard Hanson,* 34 and 7.

225. Williams, interviews of Howard Hanson. These passages are transcribed with some differences in Williams, *Conversations with Howard Hanson*, 3 and 34.

226. In David Ewen, *American Composers: A Biographical Dictionary* (New York: G. P. Putnam's Sons, 1982), 304.

CHAPTER 8
CODA: THE ELEMENTS OF STYLE

227. Burnet C. Tuthill, "Howard Hanson," *The Musical Quarterly* 22 (1936): 143, 145.

228. Louis Biancolli, "Koussevitsky Leads Howard Hanson Opus," *New York World-Telegram*, 17 January 1949: 12; Norman Nairn, "Eastman Concert Offers Highlights of Hanson Works," *Rochester Democrat and Chronicle*, 20 November 1949, section B: 11; J. Rigbie Turner, "Alice Tully Hall," *Music Journal* 30 (June 1972): 38; Nicolas Slonimsky, "Hanson, Howard" in *Dictionary of Contemporary Music*, edited by John Vinton (New York: E. P.

Dutton and Co., Inc., 1974), 299; Harold Gleason and Warren Becker, "Outline VI: Howard (Harold) Hanson," in *20th-Century American Composers*, Second Edition (Bloomington: Frangipani Press, 1980), 81, 82.

229. Paul Affelder, "Hanson Leads New Concerto in Brooklyn," *Rochester Democrat and Chronicle*, 16 January 1949, section C: 6.

230. John Tasker Howard, *Our American Music*, Fourth Edition (New York: Thomas Y. Crowell Company, 1965), 431; *International Cyclopedia of Music and Musicians*, edited by Robert Sabin (NY: Dodd, Mead and Company, 1964), 887; Gleason and Becker, *20th-Century American Composers*, 81.

231. The love duet can be found in Act II, Scene 3 of the opera. The third movement of the Suite is identical except that the vocal parts are omitted. The rehearsal numbers are the same in the opera and the Suite; the first measure of the third movement of the Suite corresponds to rehearsal 201 in the score of the opera.

232. James E. Perone, *Howard Hanson: A Bio-Bibliography* (Westport and London: Greenwood Press, 1993), 8.

233. David Russell Williams, recorded interviews of Howard Hanson (summer 1978), accession no. 000.35, Eastman School of Music Archives, Sibley Music Library, Eastman School of Music, University of Rochester, Rochester, NY. These passages are transcribed with certain differences in David Russell Williams, *Conversations with Howard Hanson* (Arkadelphia, Ark.: Delta Publications, 1988), 7, 14, 40.

234. Williams, *Conversations with Howard Hanson,* 8.

235. Hanson's actual words were, "Very heavy on major thirds, and then I did a lot with minor thirds." (This sentence is transcribed with certain differences in Williams, *Conversations with Howard Hanson*, 8.) It is unclear whether Hanson meant by this that minor thirds were also prominent in the Symphony no. 3, or that they were only prominent in later pieces. If the latter, it would have been a strange thing for him to say; as the following discussion shows clearly, minor thirds are at least as prominently featured in this symphony as are major thirds.

236. Williams, *Conversations with Howard Hanson*, 8 and 41. The sonority *pdt* is equivalent to sc 3-5 [016].

237. Ibid., 21.

238. See the citation for the Howard Hanson Papers in the Bibliography. The sketches associated with the Symphony no. 2 can be found in Box 52, Folders 1 and 5.

239. Quoted in "Howard Hanson on Music," *Howard Hanson: A Tribute* (Eastman School of Music souvenir program, 28 October 1981).

Selected Bibliography

American Composers' Concerts and Festivals of American Music 1925–1971: Cumulative Repertoire. [Edited by Charles Riker and Ruth Watanabe.] Rochester: The Institute of American Music of the University of Rochester, 1972.

Bernard, Jonathan. "Chord, Collection, and Set in Twentieth-Century Theory." In *Music Theory in Concept and Practice*, edited by James M. Baker, David W. Beach, and Jonathan W. Bernard. Rochester: University of Rochester Press, 1997.

Boatwright, Howard. Review of *Harmonic Materials of Modern Music* by Howard Hanson. *Journal of the American Musicological Society* 17 (1964): 408–13.

Cohen, Allen. "The Road Less Travelled: Howard Hanson's Set Theory." Paper delivered at annual meeting of Music Theory Society of New York State, 18–19 April 1998.

Cross, Milton, and David Ewen. "Howard Hanson." In *Milton Cross' Encyclopedia of the Great Composers and their Music*, Vol. I, 347–51. Garden City: Doubleday & Company, Inc., 1962.

Dictionary of Contemporary Music. Edited by John Vinton. New York: E. P. Dutton and Co., Inc., 1974.

The Eastman School of Music, 1947–1962. Edited by Charles Riker. Rochester: University of Rochester, 1963.

Ewen, David. "Hanson, Howard." In *American Composers: A Biographical Dictionary*, 302–05. New York: G. P. Putnam's Sons, 1982.

_____. "Howard Hanson." In *The World of Twentieth-Century Music*, 333–39. Englewood Cliffs: Prentice-Hall, Inc., 1968.

_____. "Howard Hanson." In *Composers since 1900*, 257–61. New York: The H. W. Wilson Company, 1969.

Forte, Allen. "A Theory of Set-Complexes for Music." *Journal of Music Theory* 8 (1964): 136–83.

_____. *The Structure of Atonal Music*. New Haven and London: Yale University Press, 1973.

George, Graham. Review of *Harmonic Materials of Modern Music* by Howard Hanson. *The Canadian Music Journal* 5, no. 3 (1961): 67–71.

Gleason, Harold, and Warren Becker. "Outline VI: Howard (Harold) Hanson." In *20th-Century American Composers*, 78–91. 2nd edition. Music Literature Outlines, Series IV. Bloomington: Frangipani Press, 1980.

Goss, Madeleine. "Howard Hanson." In *Modern Music-Makers*, 222–36. New York: E. P. Dutton & Company, Inc., 1952.

Hanson, Howard. "The Big Bell and the Little Bells." In *The New Scribner Music Library*, edited by Merle Montgomery, vol. 1, 86. Howard Hanson, Editor-in-Chief. New York: Charles Scribner's Sons, 1972.

_____. Concerto in G Major for Pianoforte and Orchestra, Opus 36. Full score. New York: Carl Fischer, 1948.

_____. *A Decade of Progress*. Rochester: University of Rochester, 1931.

_____. *Elegy,* Opus 44. Study score. Rochester: Eastman School of Music, University of Rochester, 1956.

_____. *For the First Time*. Piano score. New York: Carl Fischer, 1970.

_____. *Harmonic Materials of Modern Music: Resources of the Tempered Scale*. New York: Appleton-Century-Crofts, 1960.

_____. "Horn-Calls in the Forest." In *The New Scribner Music Library*, edited by Merle Montgomery, vol. 1, 87. Howard Hanson, Editor-in-Chief. New York: Charles Scribner's Sons, 1972.

_____. Howard Hanson Papers. Accession no. 997.12, Eastman School of Music Archives, Sibley Music Library, Eastman School of Music, University of Rochester, Rochester, NY. (Finding Aid prepared by Elizabeth Wells.)

_____. "The Lament for Beowulf." In *The Composer's Point of View*, edited by Robert Stephan Hines. Norman, Okl.: University of Oklahoma Press, 1963.

_____. "[Letter] To the President of the University of Rochester, and the Board of Managers of the Eastman School of Music." 1934? In Eastman School of Music Archives, call no. MT4.R67 E13L.

_____. Liner notes to *The Composer and His Orchestra Vol. II: An Analysis, with Musical Illustrations, of Howard Hanson's "Mosaics."* Eastman-Rochester Orchestra, conducted by Howard Hanson. Mercury Records MG50267 and SR 90267, 1962.

_____. Liner notes to *The Composer and His Orchestra Vol. III: An Analysis, with Musical Illustrations, of Howard Hanson's "For the First Time."* Eastman Philharmonia, conducted by Howard Hanson. Mercury Records MG50357 and SR90357, 1963.

_____. Liner notes to *Young Composer's Guide to the Six Tone Scale*. Eastman Wind Ensemble, conducted by Donald Hunsberger. Mercury Records (Golden Imports) SRI 75132, 1978.

_____. *Merry Mount* Suite. Miniature score. New York: Harms, 1938.

_____. *Mosaics*. Full score. New York: Carl Fischer, 1958.

_____. *Montgomery Lectures on Contemporary Civilization: Music in Con-temporary American Civilization.* Lincoln: University of Nebraska, 1951.

_____. *Nymph and Satyr.* Full score. New York: Carl Fischer, 1979.

_____. Recorded oral analysis of *For the First Time* and *Mosaics.* On *The Composer and His Orchestra.* Eastman-Rochester Orchestra and East-man Philharmonia, conducted by Howard Hanson. Mercury/Polygram compact discs 434 370-2, 1996.

_____. *A Sea Symphony* (Symphony no 7). Full score. New York: Carl Fischer, 1977.

_____. *Sinfonia Sacra* (Symphony no. 5), Opus 43. Full score. Rochester: Eastman School of Music, 1955.

_____. Symphony no. 2, Opus 30. Study score. New York: Carl Fischer, 1932.

_____. Symphony no. 3, Opus 33. Full score. Rochester: Eastman School of Music, 1938.

_____. Symphony no. 6. Study score. New York: Carl Fischer, 1968.

_____. "Tricks or Treats." In *The New Scribner Music Library*, edited by Merle Montgomery, vol. 1, 87. Howard Hanson, Editor-in-Chief. New York: Charles Scribner's Sons, 1972.

_____. *Two Decades of Progress.* Rochester: University of Rochester, 1941.

_____. *Young Person's Guide to the Six-Tone Scale.* Full score. New York: Carl Fischer Inc., 1995.

Howard, John Tasker. *Our American Music: A Comprehensive History from 1620 to the Present.* Fourth Edition. New York: Thomas Y. Crowell Company, 1965.

Jackson, David Lowell. "Horizontal and Vertical Analysis Data Extraction Using a Computer Program." Ph.D. diss., University of Cincinnati, 1981.

Janes, Jean Karole. "From North and West to a Concerto for Organ, Strings, and Harp: An Examination of Howard Hanson's Compositional Style Through a Study of Revisions." Master's thesis, University of Rochester, 1981.

Kalyn, Andrea Sherlock. "Constructing a Nation's Music: Howard Hanson's American Composers' Concerts and Festivals of American Music, 1925–71." Ph.D. diss., University of Rochester, 2001.

Lenti, Vincent A. "The Eastman School of Music." *Rochester History* 58 (1996): 3–31.

Lloyd, Norman. Review of *Harmonic Materials of Modern Music* by Howard Hanson. *Journal of Research in Music Education* 8, no. 2 (1960): 128-30.

Machlis, Joseph. "Howard Hanson." In *Introduction to Contemporary Music*, 545–6. New York: W. W. Norton & Company Inc., 1961.

Mitchell, William J. Review of *Harmonic Materials of Modern Music* by Howard Hanson. *Journal of Music Theory* 4 (1960): 236–43.

Monroe, Robert C. "Howard Hanson: American Music Educator." Ph.D. diss., Florida State University, 1970.

Moomaw, Charles Jay. "A PL/1 Program for the Harmonic Analysis of Music by the Theories of Paul Hindemith and Howard Hanson." Master's the-sis, University of Cincinnati, 1973.

Parker, Mark Mason. "Classification of Pitch Materials in Three Compositions by Howard Hanson." Master's thesis, Eastman School of Music, 1976.

Perle, George. *Serial Composition and Atonality*. 6th edition. Berkeley: University of California Press, 1991.

Perone, James E. *Howard Hanson: A Bio-Bibliography*. Westport and London: Greenwood Press, 1993.

Plain, Marilyn V. *Howard Hanson: A Comprehensive Catalog of the Manuscripts*. Rochester: Eastman School of Music Press, 1997.

Rahn, John. *Basic Atonal Theory*. New York: Schirmer Books, 1980.

Riker, Charles. *The Eastman School of Music: Its First Quarter Century, 1921–1946*. Rochester: University of Rochester, 1948.

Royce, Edward. "Howard Hanson." In *American Composers on American Music: A Symposium*, edited by Henry Cowell, 97–100. New York: Frederick Ungar, 1962.

Schmalfeldt, Janet. *Berg's "Wozzeck": Harmonic Language and Dramatic Design*. New Haven: Yale University Press, 1983.

Simmons, Walter. *Voices in the Wilderness: Six American Neo-Romantic Composers*. Lanham, MD: Scarecrow Press, 2003.

Slonimsky, Nicolas. Review of *Harmonic Materials of Modern Music* by Howard Hanson. *Notes* 18 (1961): 415–16.

_____. "Hanson, Howard (Harold)." In *Baker's Biographical Dictionary of Musicians*. 8th Edition. New York: Schirmer Books/Macmillan, Inc., 1992.

Straus, Joseph N. *Introduction to Post-Tonal Theory*. 2nd edition. Upper Saddle River, NJ: Prentice Hall, 2000.

Sutton, Robert. "Howard Hanson, Set Theory Pioneer." *Sonus* 8, no. 1 (fall 1987): 17–39.

Tawa, Nicholas E. *Serenading the Reluctant Eagle*. New York: Schirmer Books, 1984.

Thomson, Virgil. *American Music Since 1910*. New York: Holt, Rinehart and Winston, 1971.

Tuthill, Burnet C. "Howard Hanson." *The Musical Quarterly* 22 (1936): 140–53.

Watanabe, Ruth T. "Hanson, Howard (Harold)." In *The New Grove Dictionary of American Music*, edited by H. Wiley Hitchcock and Stanley Sadie, vol. 2, 320–22. London: Macmillan Press Limited, 1986.

_____. "Howard Hanson's Autographs in the Sibley Music Library." *Notes* 7 (March 1950): 240–42.

_____, and James Perone. "Hanson, Howard (Harold)." In *The New Grove Dictionary of Music and Musicians*, edited by Stanley Sadie and John Tyrrell, vol. 10, 833–34. London and New York: Macmillan Publishers Limited, 2001.

Werlé, Frederick. Review of *Harmonic Materials of Modern Music* by Howard Hanson. *Musical Courier* 161, no. 5 (1960): 46.

Williams, David Russell. *Conversations with Howard Hanson*. Arkadelphia, Ark.: Delta Publications, 1988.

_____. "Howard Hanson (1896–1981)." *Perspectives of New Music* 20 (1981): 12–25.

_____. Recorded interviews of Howard Hanson, summer 1978. Currently on audio cassette tapes. Accession no. 000.35, Eastman School of Music

Archives, Sibley Music Library, Eastman School of Music, University of Rochester, Rochester, NY.

Winham, Godfrey. Review of *Harmonic Materials of Modern Music* by Howard Hanson. *Perspectives of New Music* 1 (1963): 146–47.

Witucki, Alan Philip. "Thematic Transformation and Other Considerations in the Six Symphonies of Howard Hanson." Master's thesis, Michigan State University, 1978.

Index

ABOUT THE AUTHOR

Allen Cohen is Assistant Professor of Music at Fairleigh Dickinson University. He is active as a composer, theorist, conductor, and pianist in the New York City area.